Silent dark and
restless umber
gr g
sedge stained
ochre brown

WHITEWASH AND BROWN PAINT
- LOVELY -
The sketchbooks of Percy Kelly

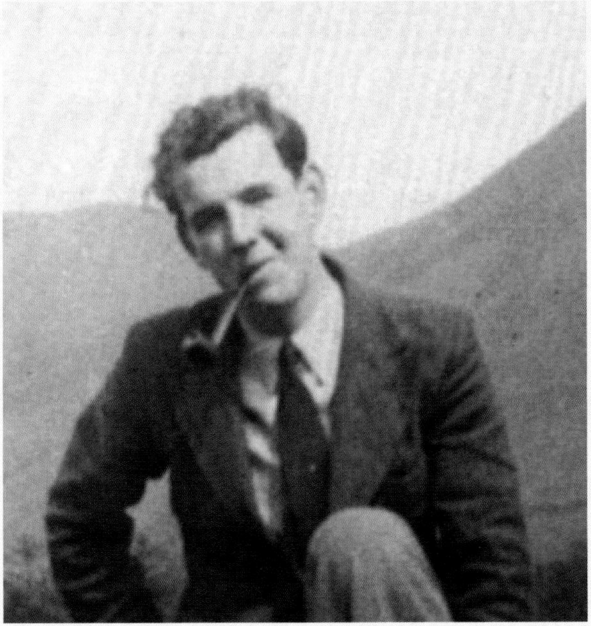

'The mass of men live lives of quiet desperation' Henry Thoreau

WHITEWASH AND BROWN PAINT - LOVELY

The sketchbooks of Percy Kelly

Chris Wadsworth.

Written and edited by
Chris Wadsworth
CASTLEGATE HOUSE

First published 2007
Castlegate House
Cockermouth Cumbria
01900 822149
gallery@castlegatehouse,co.uk
www.castlegatehouse.co.uk

Printed by Reeds Printers Ltd, Penrith Cumbria

ISBN 978-0-9555142-0-3

Other publications by the same author
The Painted letters of Percy Kelly
Sheila Fell 1931 - 1939
Winifred Nicholson; A Cumbrian Odyssey

FOREWORD

In the late summer of 1993, I took delivery of the life's work of artist Percy Kelly. It came from his cottage in Norfolk after his death on July 3rd in a cacophony of containers - mainly unframed - in large wooden bread trays in random order. Very few of the works were dated or titled which made cataloguing the collection a challenge

Percy had always been reluctant to let go of any work in his lifetime. Though desperately poor, he needed to hold on to everything he had created which meant that there were more than fifty years of drawing and painting on that delivery van. For me it was a rare opportunity to see a complete body of work by a single artist spanning his whole lifetime.

Percy's only son Brian inherited the estate and his instruction to me was to sell everything. As a factory worker who had had no contact with his father for twenty four years, he did not share his father's retentive nature with regard to art.

To begin with everything was photographed and catalogued but when things were framed for the first exhibition, I realised that I would have to give each work a title. Some of the landscapes were instantly recognisable which was easy and others could be given more general, descriptive titles such as *Windy Day* or *Church on the hill.*

As the years went by further small collections were added from various sources with the odd sketch book containing clues to places and dates of the works. *I*t wasn't until after the death of his greatest friend Joan David in 2000, when I had access to her huge collection of painted letters, that I was able to place many more of the works and learn the stories about them.

Then last year, in topsy-turvey fashion, the last pieces of the jigsaw came my way with a collection of his sketchbooks to add to the ones I already had. I found these fascinating. I could track his life and progress through them. I gained not only more specific topographical details of the paintings and drawings with which I was so familiar by now, but also an insight into his development as an artist and his way of working. It was interesting to see how he recorded information in a sketch and then honed it down in the painting often changing the composition to make a better picture. Some of the sketchbooks were made on one particular day or trip which meant I could follow his movements and mentally and sometimes physically trace his steps. In many cases I could link the preliminary sketches, the finished painting and a reference to it in the letters to Joan.

His remarkable ability to draw unerringly - to get it right first time - is impressive.

It has taken several years of research and cross-referencing to gain the full story. Only a small sample is illustrated here. There is enough material to fill several volumes.

In this book I have tried to bring these things together in a coherent way. I have shown the finished paintings alongside the sketches with Percy's notes where relevant.

Chris Wadsworth

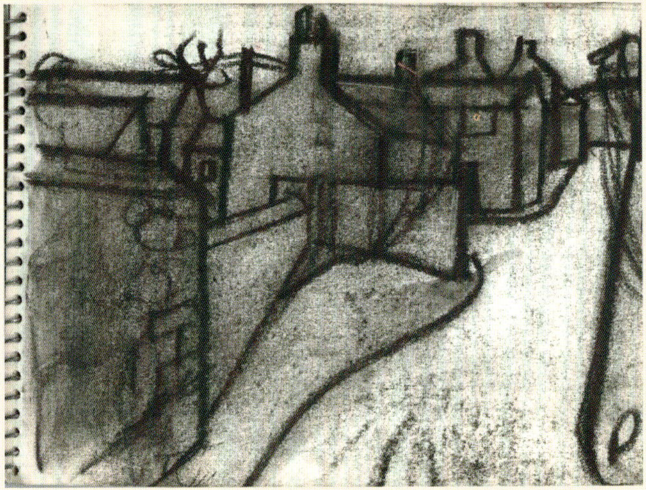

Drawing is harder work than watercolour
It is the whole picture minus the colour
The function of the drawing is the outline
The forms indicate light and shade, and make
Possible a rapid description of the scene.
Raoul Dufy

PERCY KELLY'S SKETCHBOOKS

Percy Kelly could draw as soon as he could hold a pencil. It was a talent he was born with. He and his twin brother John were 19 when they joined the Border Regiment in 1939 but Percy was soon transferred to the Royal Signals when his talent was spotted. He drew maps and diagrams for the army and came to Churchill's attention when posted in his bunker in Whitehall. When Churchill couldn't sleep, he would wander along to Percy's room, sit on his bed and talk about art.

Kelly filled many sketchbooks during the war as well as sending illustrated letters back to his young wife Audrey in Workington but sadly these weren't kept. Only one 1940 sketchbook has survived and has some very fine drawings in it. When Percy was posted to Repton, he got to know the art master at the public school and for the first time was exposed to art books and proper materials. At home he was one of seven children in a strongly religious family so the only book in the house was the Bible and the only things on the walls were religious tracts so this was a revelation. Later in London during the war years, he visited those galleries still open and began to study artists he admired.

At the end of the war he came back to work in Kendal for the Post Office and joined the Lake Artists' Society. There are several sketchbooks full of watercolours of the prettier parts of the Lake District. These watercolours are pleasant and technically very good but lack strength and definition. They laid down the rules of light, shade, recession and texture that he would use in the future. From the time that he married in 1942, he had access to a car so he could travel extensively to draw and paint. The range of his travels is shown in his 1957 sketchbook. He painted almost everything he saw.

1958 was the turning point. He became depressed and dissatisfied with his life. He needed to make progress and that meant change. In the next sketchbook he exchanged pencil for charcoal and his fine brush for one with a broader sweep. The sketches bear witness to a time of phenomenal activity. He roamed the county feverishly making drawings and notes which were then translated into a powerful set of charcoal drawings on much larger A2 paper.

Charges to pay

s. d.

RECEIVED

Delivery and Charges: Taken out by ... at ... m. Returned at ... m. (Name)

Means ... Art ... Collected ...

Distance ... Paid Out ...

Prefix. Time handed in. Office of Origin and Service Instructions. Words.

No. ...

OFFICE STAMP

At ... m

From ...

A factor that is overlooked in the teaching
of art is the training to search for colour.
I find that I am seeing colour with such
intensity that it is making it difficult for
me to adjust my physical colour sense.
It is a wonderful experience and were I not
an artist it would give me untold pleasure.
But I can never walk the countryside relaxed I
am for ever searching and my mind races along
like a turbulent mountain stream. Perhaps
like the stream I shall find peace when the water flows
more placid.

(6434) 9/52 A.O.St.

On this Post Office receipt docket at that time he wrote the following

ART

A factor that is overlooked in the teaching of art is the training to search for colour. I find that I am seeing colour with such intensity that it is making it difficult for me to adjust my physical colour sense. It is a wonderful experience and were I not an artist it would give me untold pleasure. But I can never walk the countryside relaxed. I am forever searching and my mind races along like a turbulent mountain stream. Perhaps like the stream I shall find peace when the water flows more placid

I have to condense my energies as it were into one single day. There are countless ideas in my mind and my greatest difficulty is how to collect and concentrate all my efforts to a single purpose so my work differs each time I pick up my brush,

After this frantic and productive bout of activity, Percy decided to go to Art College and his wife Audrey became the major wage earner. The interviewing committee thought that at the mature age of 42 he could be out of his depth among the young talent and declined to give him a grant until he had proved himself. They needn't have worried, he held his own. The sketchbooks made during his 4 years at the college bear witness to this. Until then he had no desire to draw or paint the human figure but exercises were set by his tutors and he was launched into Carlisle and told to draw people in public places. We can almost trace his steps from the notebooks. He spent a lot of time on Carlisle Station, in the market and around garages and building sites. There is no doubt that he could draw people as well as he drew places but once his days at the college were over, he didn't draw people again - he saw the landscape paintings as an abstract arrangement of shapes - the human body or animals would spoil the composition. As an examination piece, he made a huge painting in one day on Carlisle station. He recounts in a letter to Joan David years later, that on his return to college he was accused of cheating. The tutor alleged it must have taken him more than the one day allotted time. Percy handed the painting in and never saw it again. This is either true, partially true or the beginning of his paranoia.

There is one particularly thick notebook of 60 small plates made in 1964 which is packed with ideas. These were the beginnings of major themes which then ran through his work for the rest of his life. A large part of that particular book is reproduced here as it is so beautiful and so important.

On leaving college in 1965 he became a full time artist and never went into paid employment again. He was very prolific, filling sketchbook after sketchbook with drawings of the West Cumbrian coast and its harbours, the industrial scene and the inland villages. His favourite places were Maryport, West Newton, Allonby where he lived and Whitehaven, particularly Parton. In the countryside, he loved the Vale of Lorton - Loweswater, Buttermere and Crummock Water above all . It is interesting to compare his earlier sketches of these places with the later sketches and the big paintings.

In 1964, he won a travelling scholarship and opted to go to Brittany. He had been in France during the war and wanted to return. Although there are quite a lot of drawings and paintings of Brittany, there are no sketchbooks in evidence as such. Maybe they will turn up one day. There are however many sketchbooks of his annual visits to Cornwall where he taught in a summer school run by Charles Breaker in St Ives. His love of boats and harbours came to the fore - he must have been in his element down there.
His 7 years in Pembrokeshire were not so productive. It was not a happy time with increasing gender confusion. His retentiveness over his work was becoming acute and a major dispute with neighbours in St Davids over his efforts to build an extension to house his second wife and 3 step children obsessed him.
He was by now suffering with a marked and acute personality disorder. He doggedly tried to do all the building and car maintenance work himself - a major task with a near derelict building and very old cars.
Chris was very supportive and helped with the building work but got very frustrated at the constant breaking down of the poorly maintained old vehicles. They were sitting on a collection of extremely saleable and valuable work which would have solved all their financial problems and allowed them to employ builders and buy a decent car but Percy refused. He was cross dressing much of the time so, with their social life difficult and their finances in a serious state, they moved to Norfolk and Christine left him.
His last years in Norfolk yield very little in the way of sketchbooks. All his energies were taken up with his marriage breakdown and gender change as well as the ongoing car maintenance and DIY projects. He never stopped drawing and painting but his illustrated letters to Joan David and other friends with the accompanying drawings and diagrams served the same purpose. This also was a time when he was dreadfully homesick for his native county and justified his years of retentiveness by sifting through his Cumbrian drawings and sketches and making some fine paintings from them.
These sketchbooks and associated paintings bear witness to a sad, lonely and highly talented man.

Chris Wadsworth January 2007

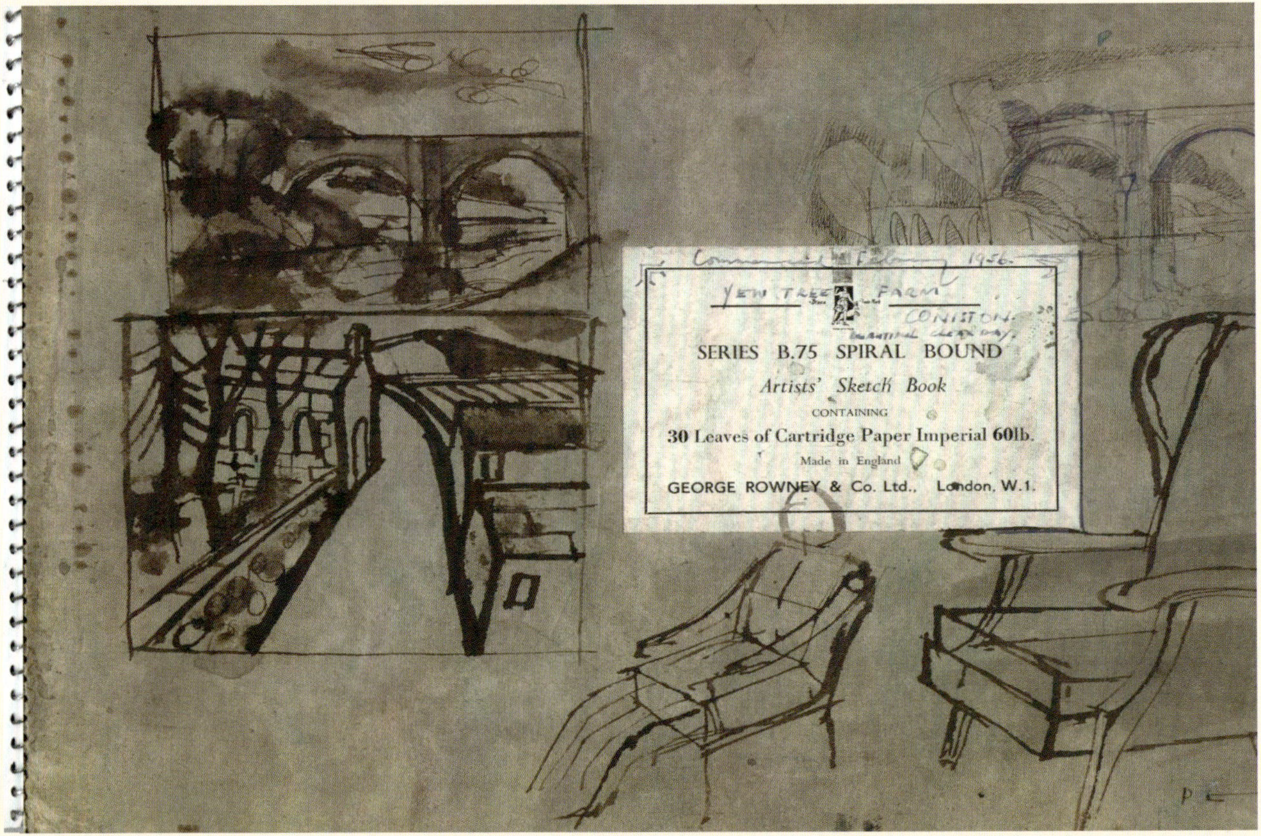

Sketch book cover 1956

EARLY DRAWINGS AND PAINTINGS

Since his school days through his work for the Post Office and during the war, Percy was building on his remarkable natural drawing ability and developing observation skills. Totally untaught, these early sketch books illustrate his mastery of light and shade, colour and form.

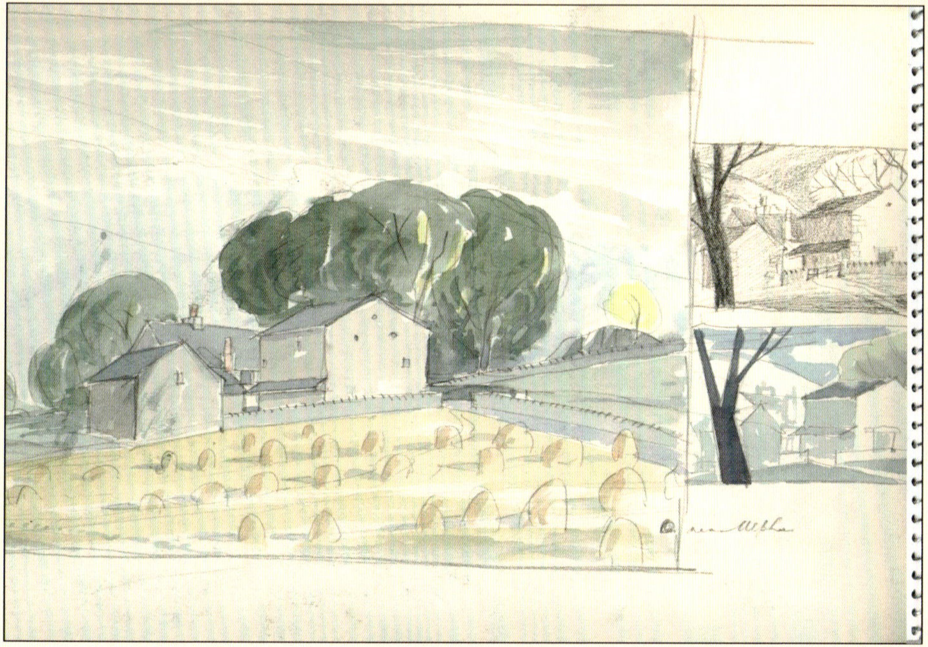

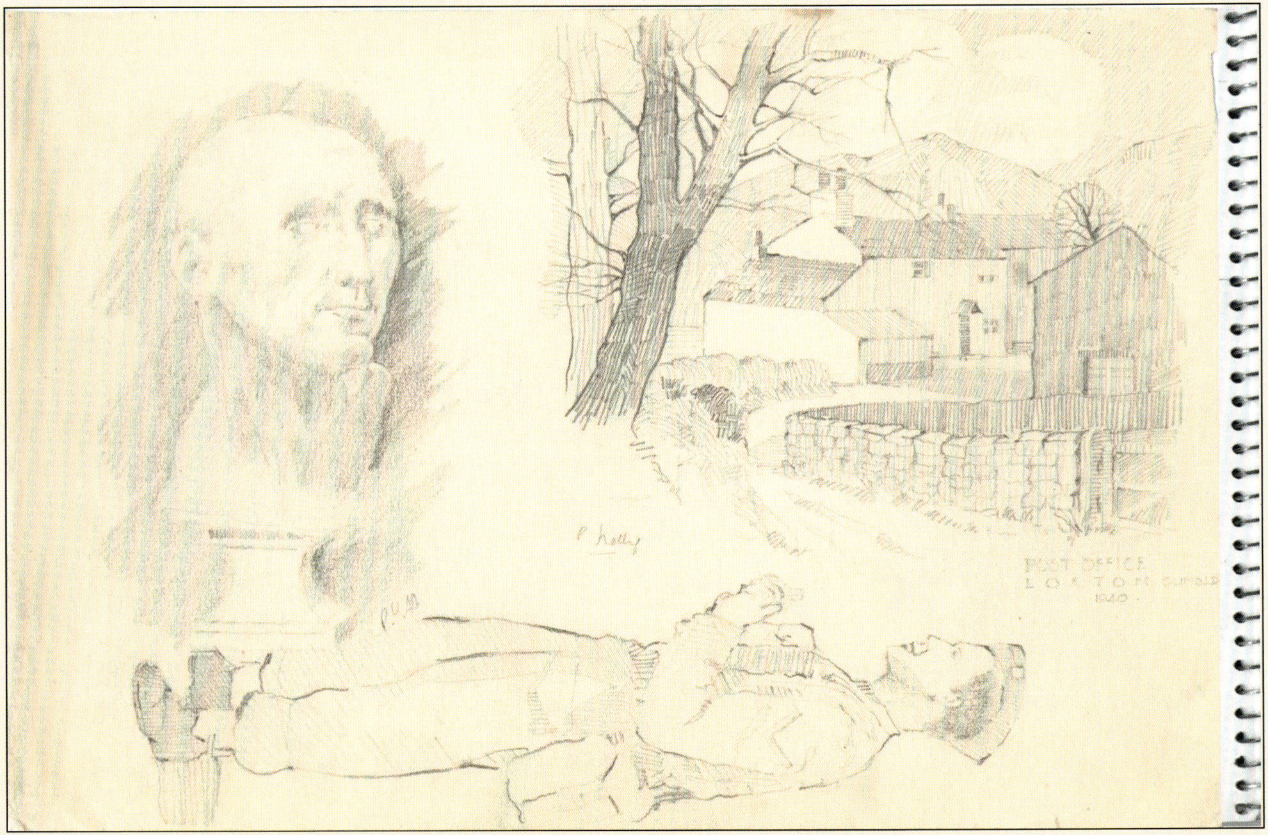

1940

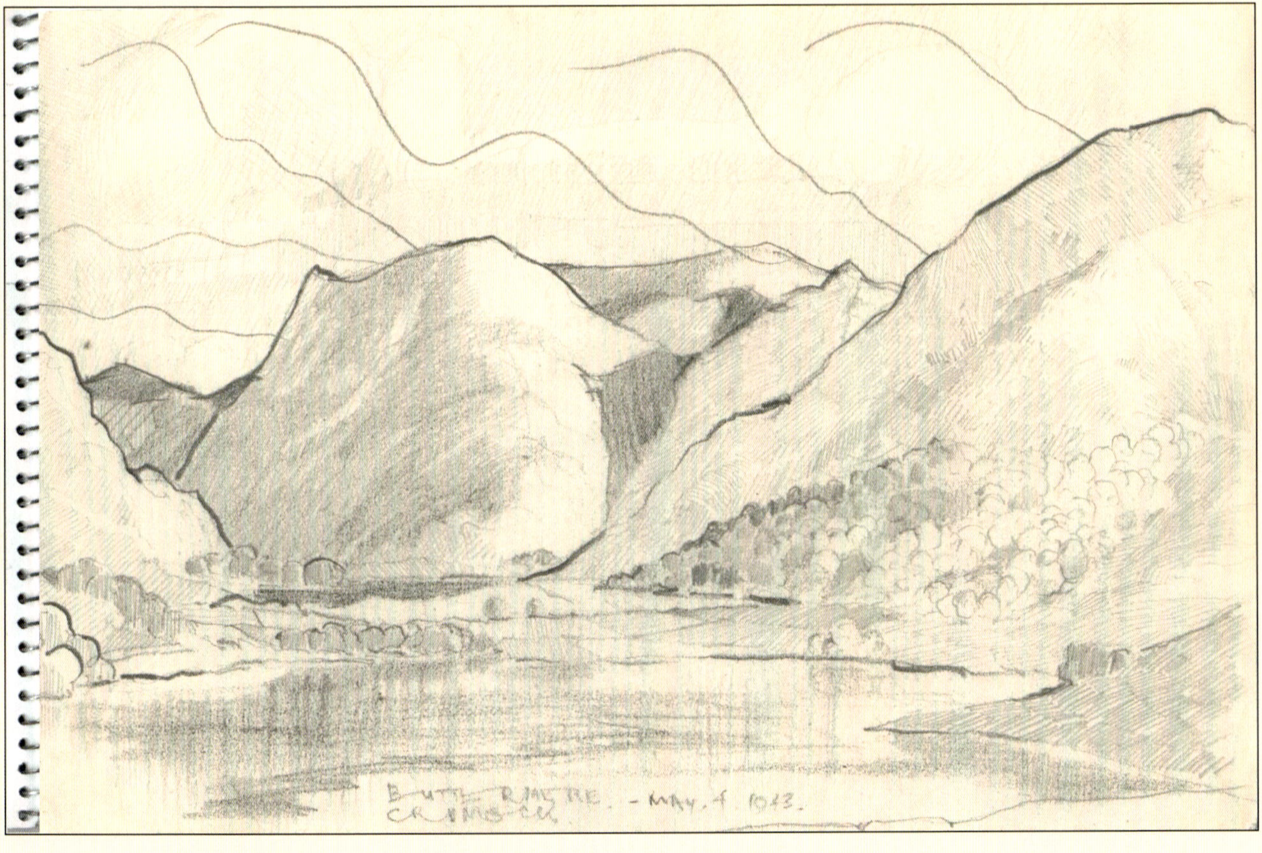

Buttermere, Crummock May 4th 1948

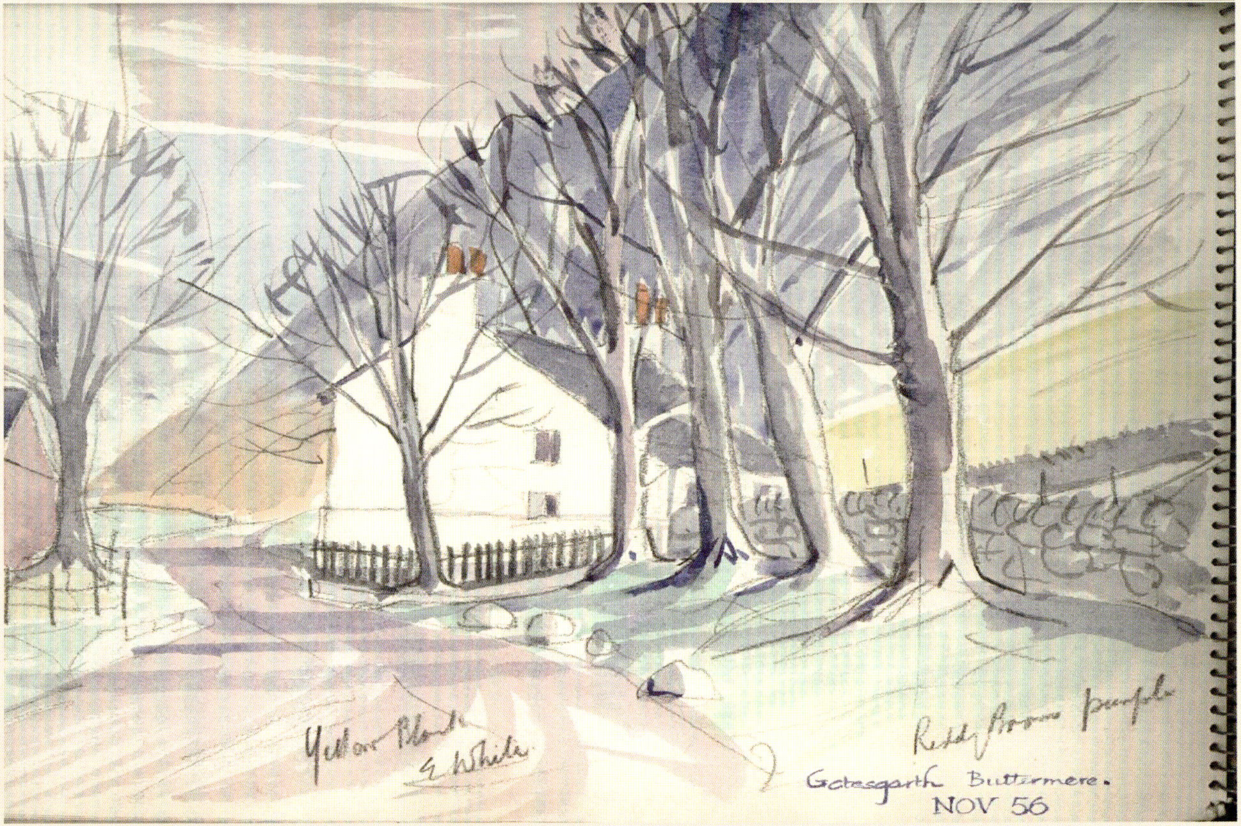

Gatescarth, Buttermere November 1956

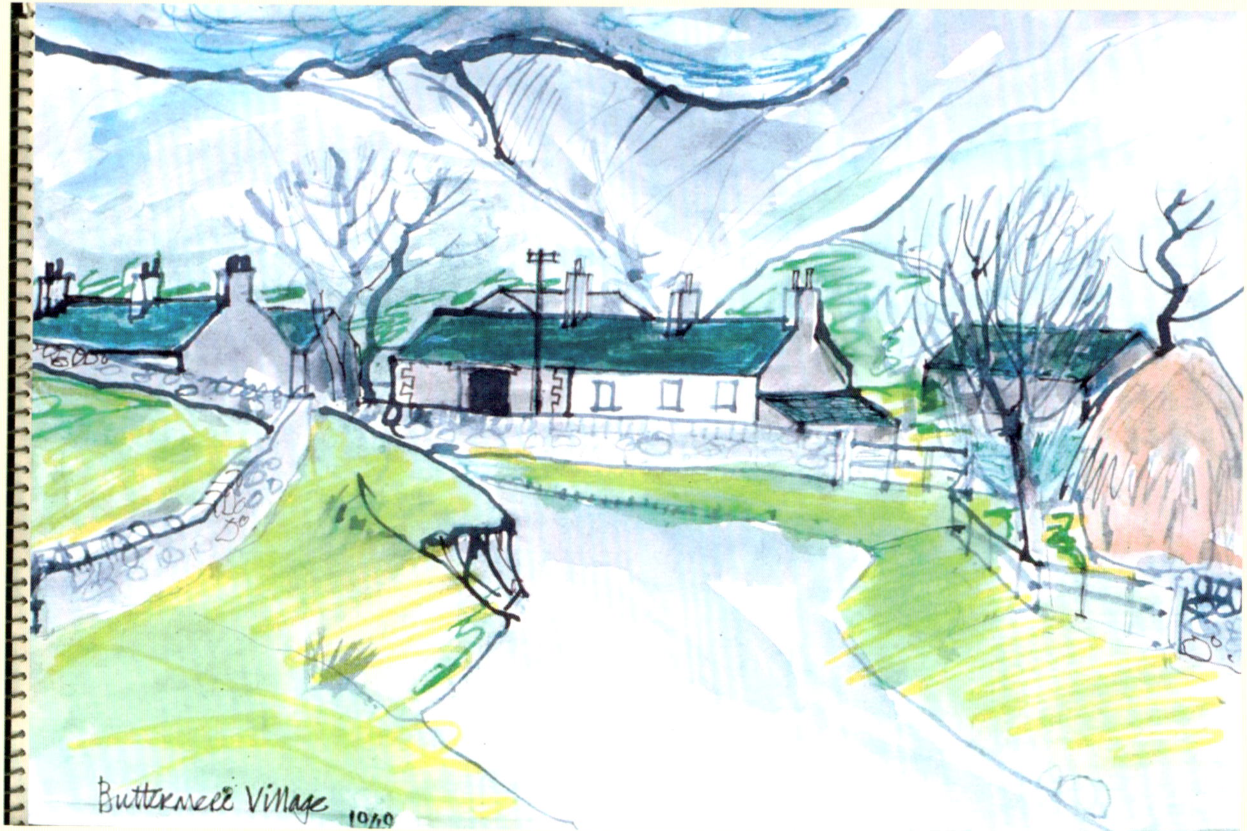

Buttermere Village 1960

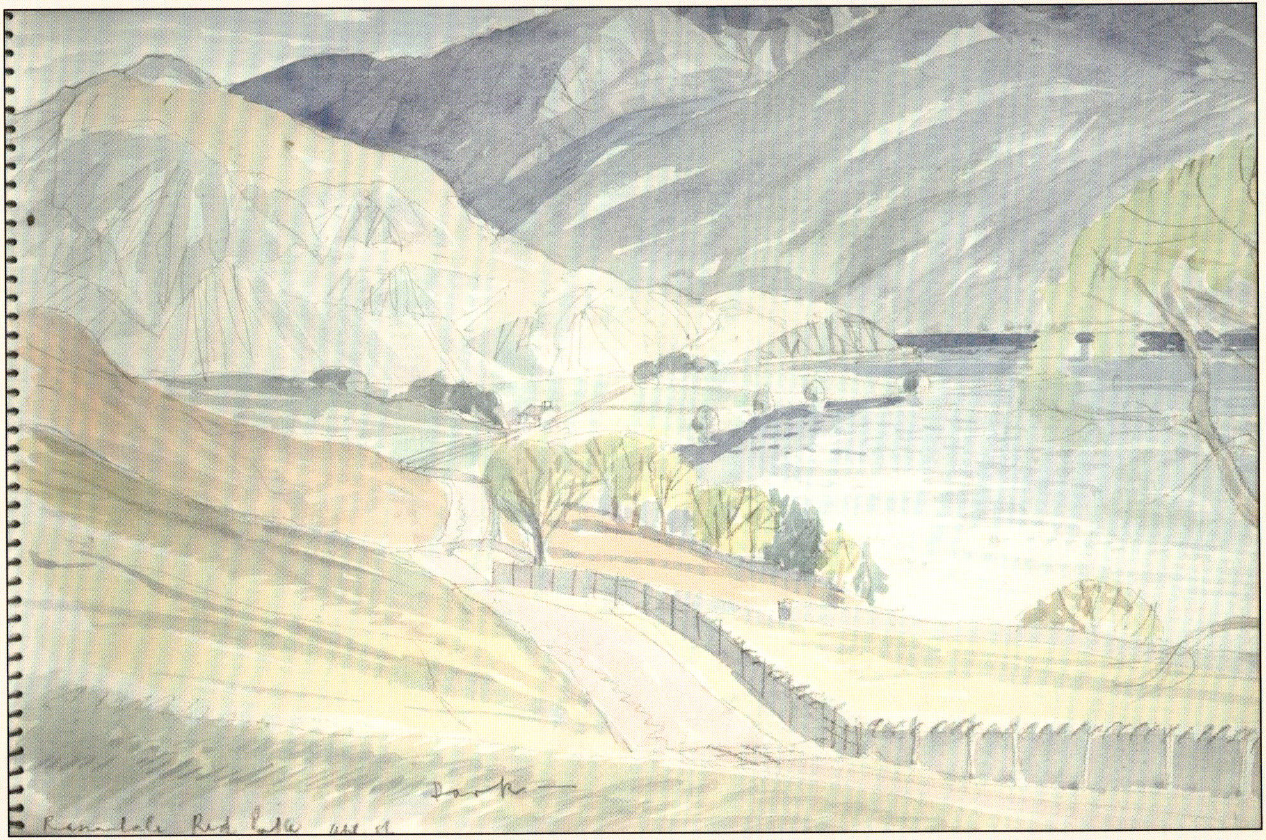

Rannerdale, Red Pike April 1956

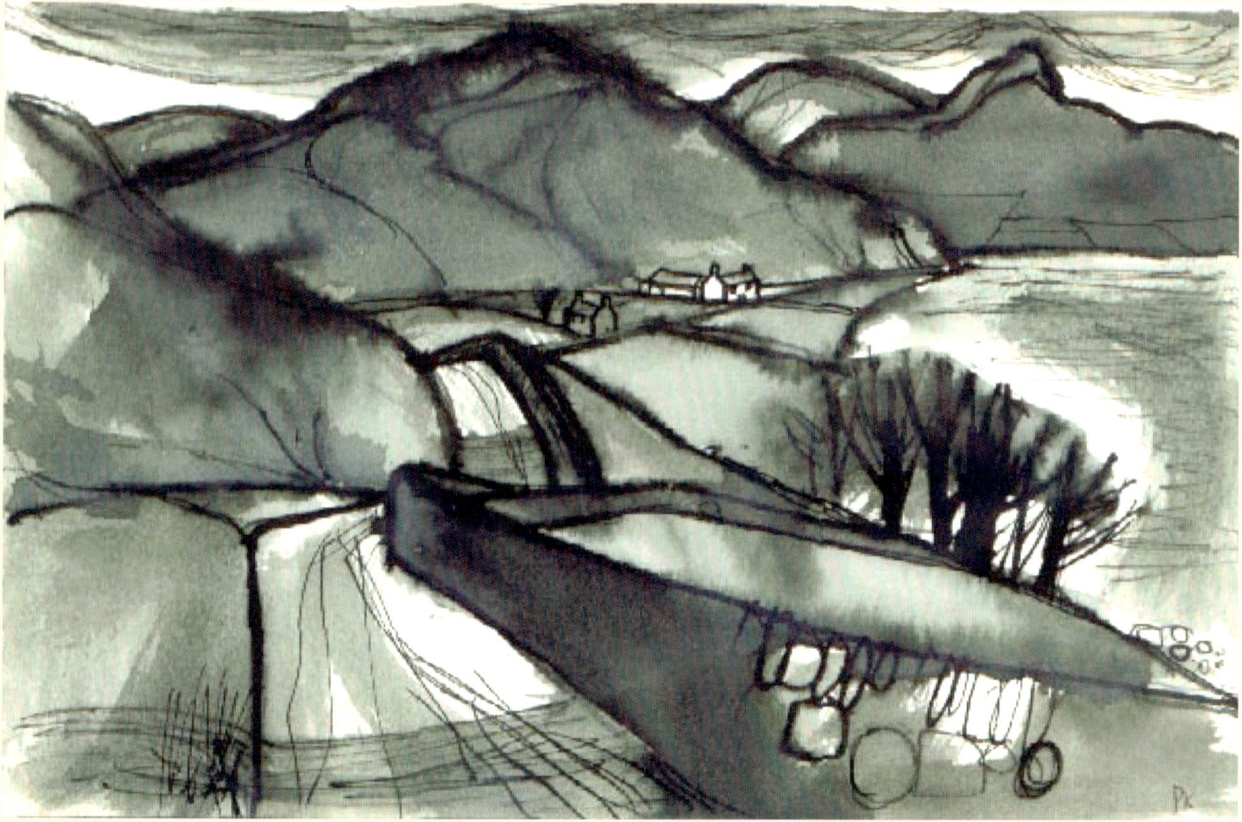

Crummock Water; Watercolour c1970

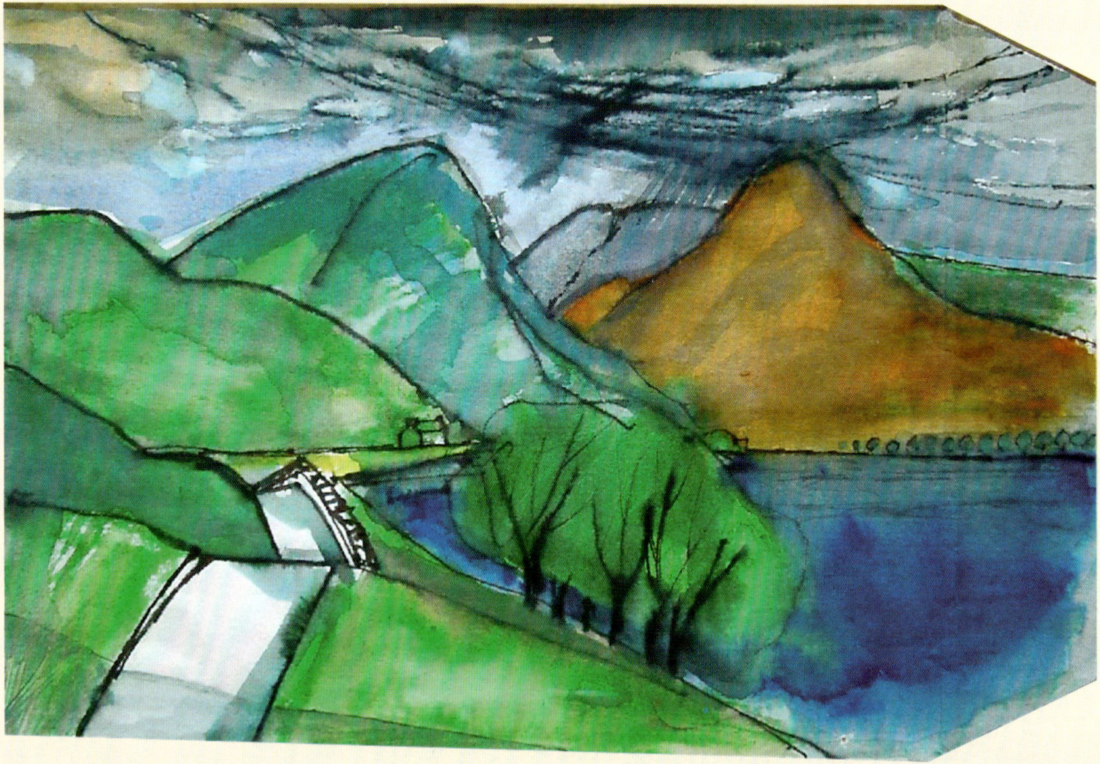

A5 envelope of the same view sent to Joan David 1986 with a painted letter inside.
It was placed inside an A4 envelope so as not to spoil it with the address

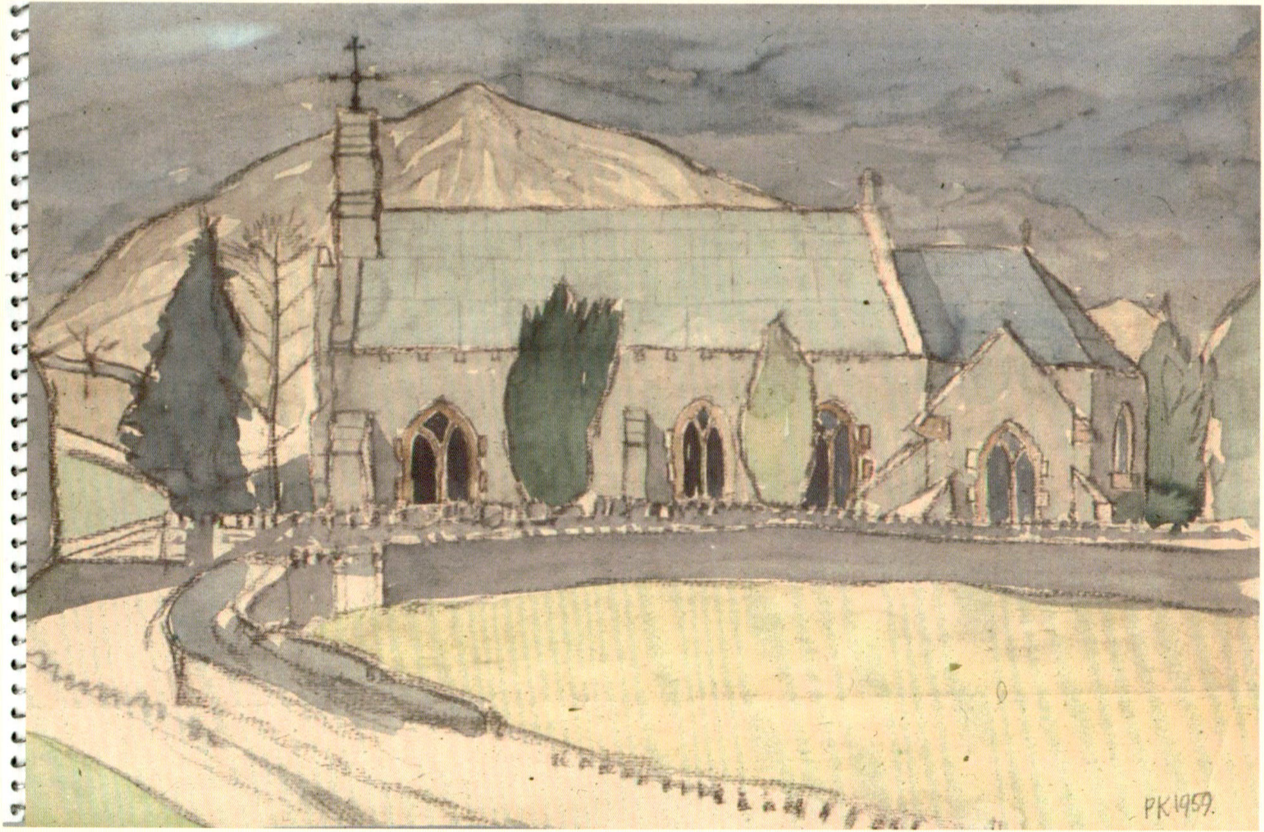

Loweswater Church from the East 1959

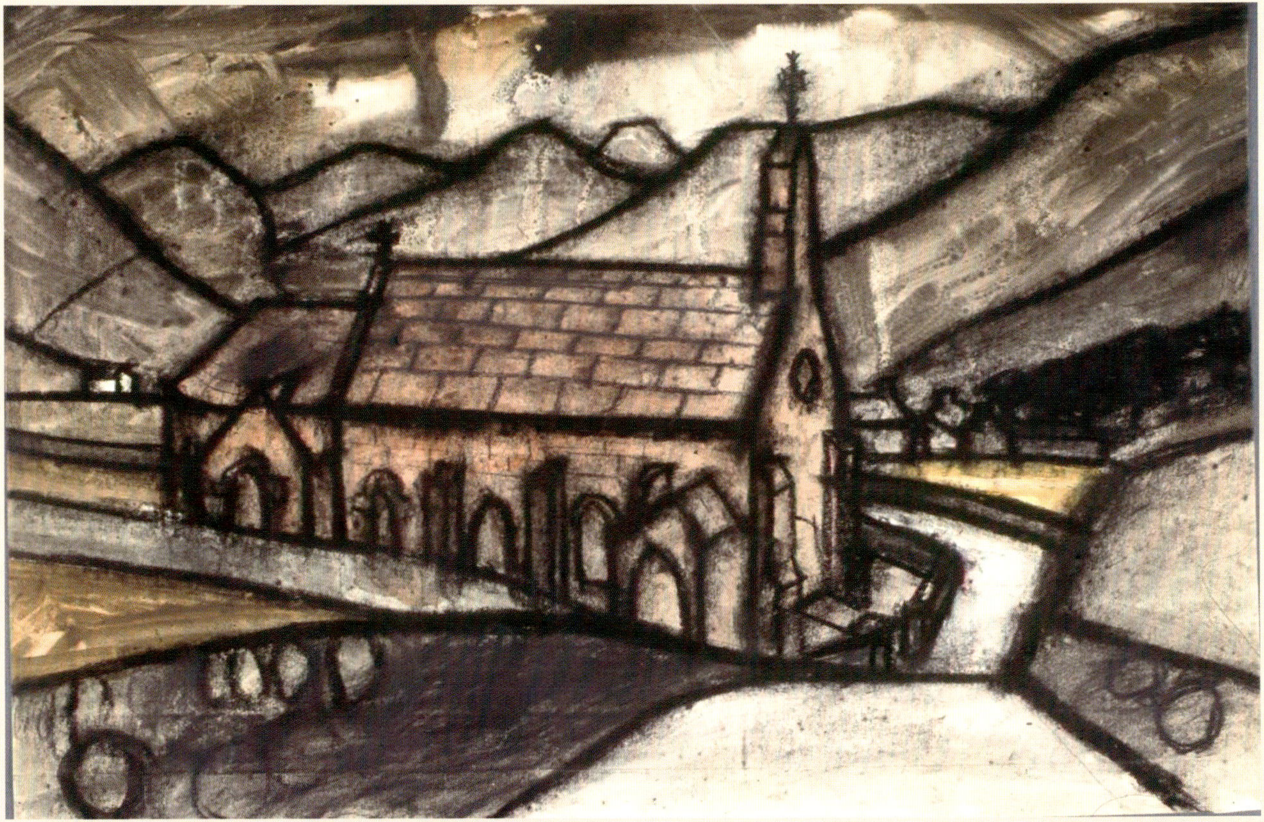

Loweswater Church; charcoal/watercolour c 1965

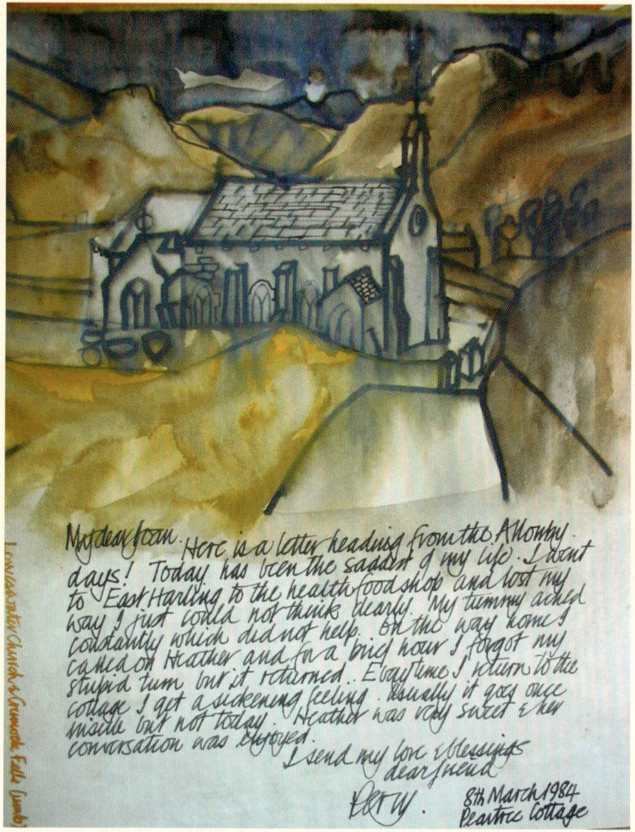
My dear Joan. Here is a letter heading from the Allonby days! Today has been the saddest of my life. I went to East Harling to the health food shop and lost my way I just could not think clearly. My tummy ached constantly which did not help. On the way home I called on Heather and for a brief hour I forgot my stupid tum but it returned.. Everytime I return to the cottage I get a sickening feeling. Usually it goes once inside but not today. Heather was very sweet & her conversation was enjoyed.

I send my love & blessings dear friend

Percy. 8th March 1984 Peartree Cottage

Loweswater Church & Crummock Fells (Cumb)

Letter to Joan David
Written after his second wife Christine had left him

Loweswater Church and Crummock Fells, Cumberland

My dear Joan

Here is a letterheading from the Allonby days. Today has been the saddest of my life.. I went to East Harling to the health food shop and lost my way. I just could not think clearly. My tummy ached constantly which did not help. On the way home I called on Heather and for a brief hour forgot my stupid tum but it returned. Every time I return to the cottage I get a sickening feeling. Usually it goes once inside but not today. Heather was very sweet and her conversation was enjoyed.

I send my love and blessings dear friend

Percy

8th March 1984

Pear Tree Cottage

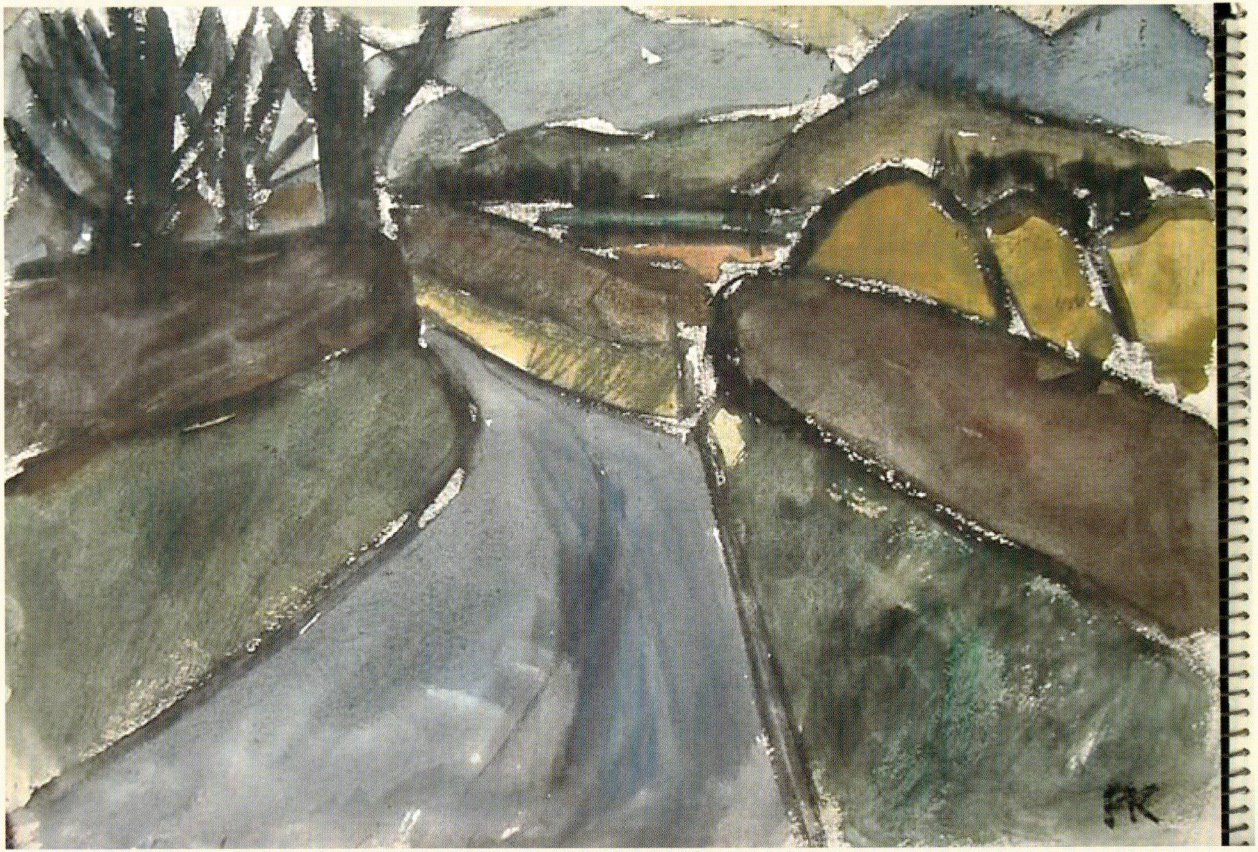

Haystacks near Loweswater 1956

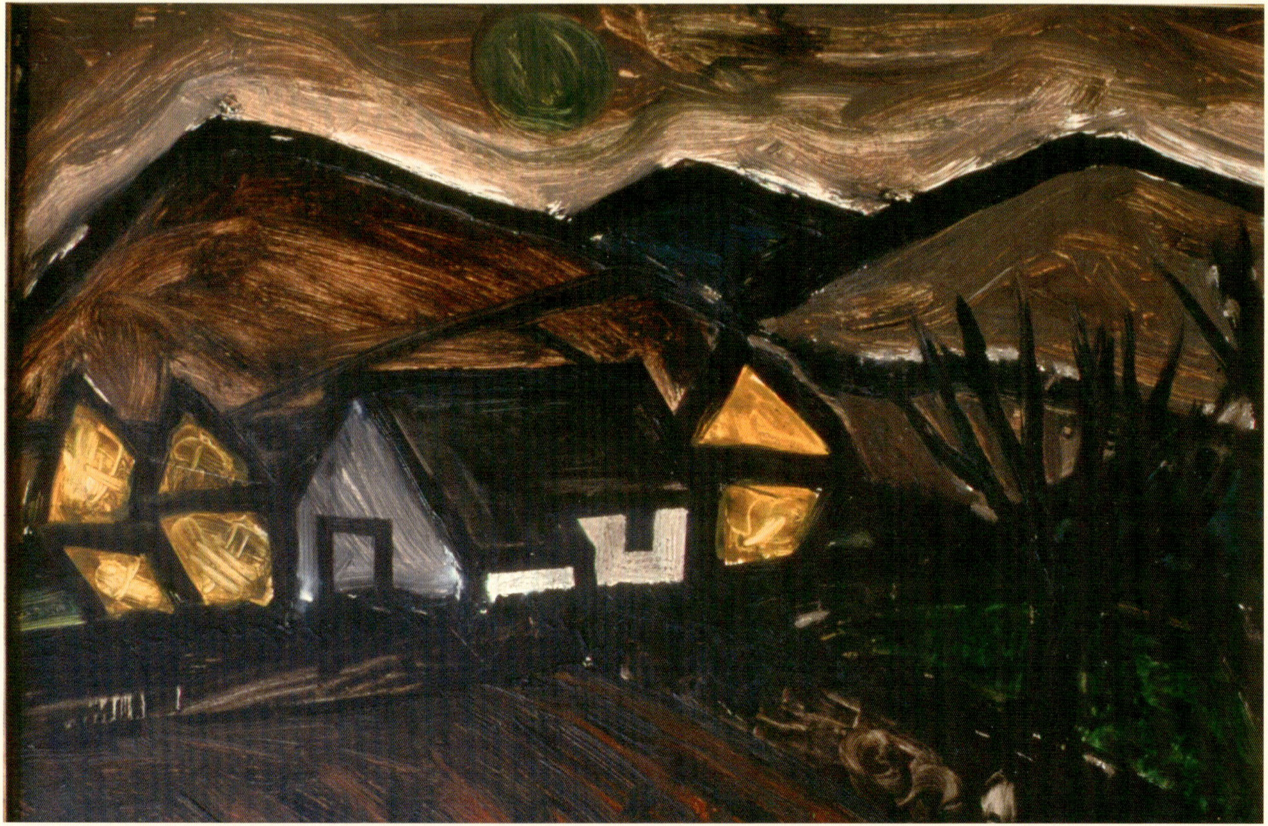

Haystacks Vale of Lorton Oil on board c 1967

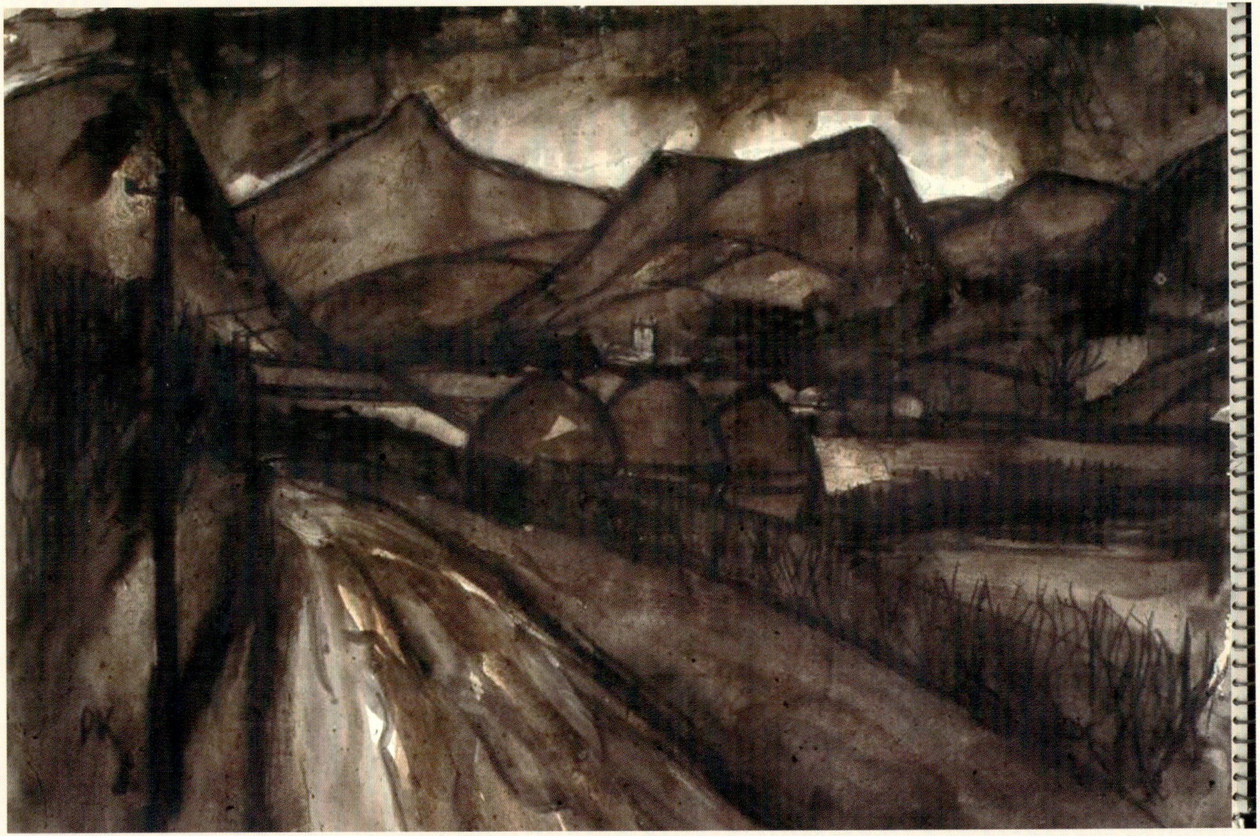

Haystacks Vale of Lorton; Charcoal/watercolour c 1964

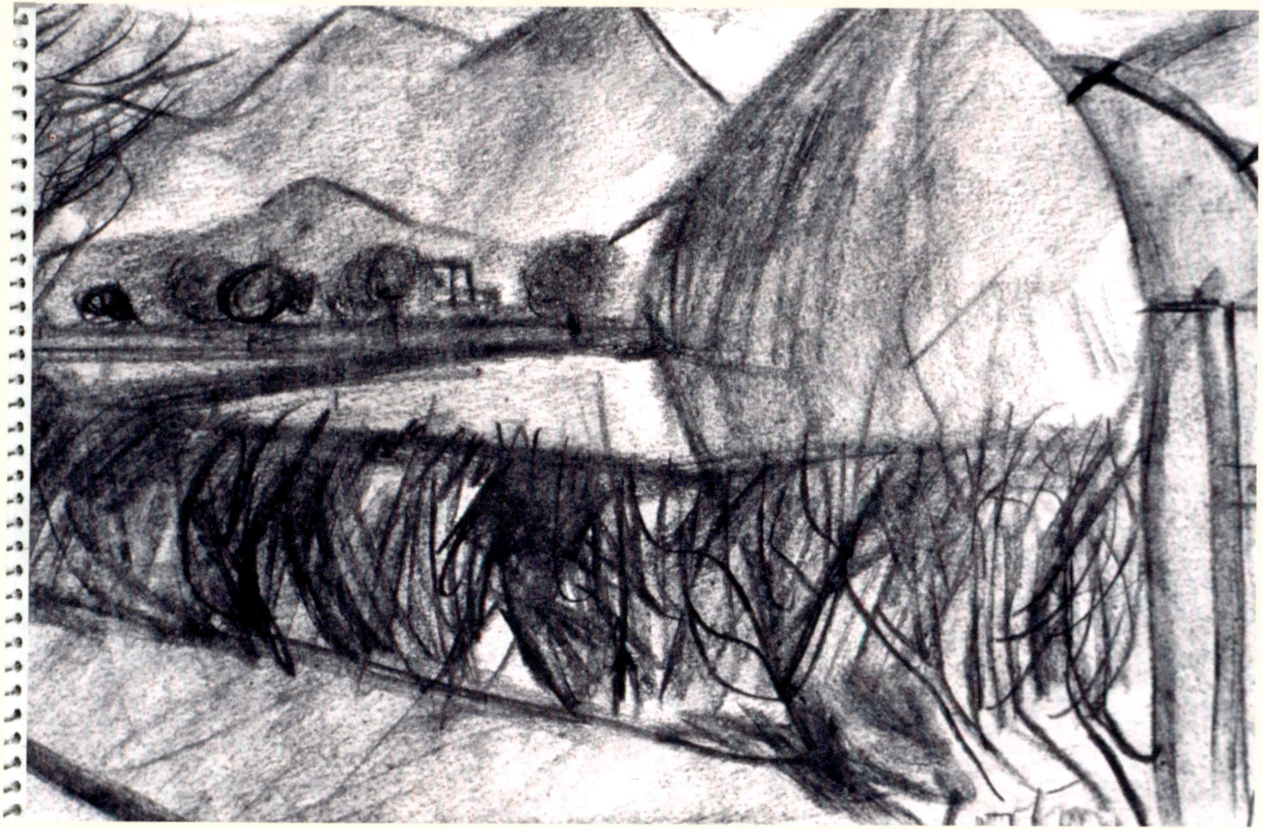

Lorton; Charcoal drawing c 1958

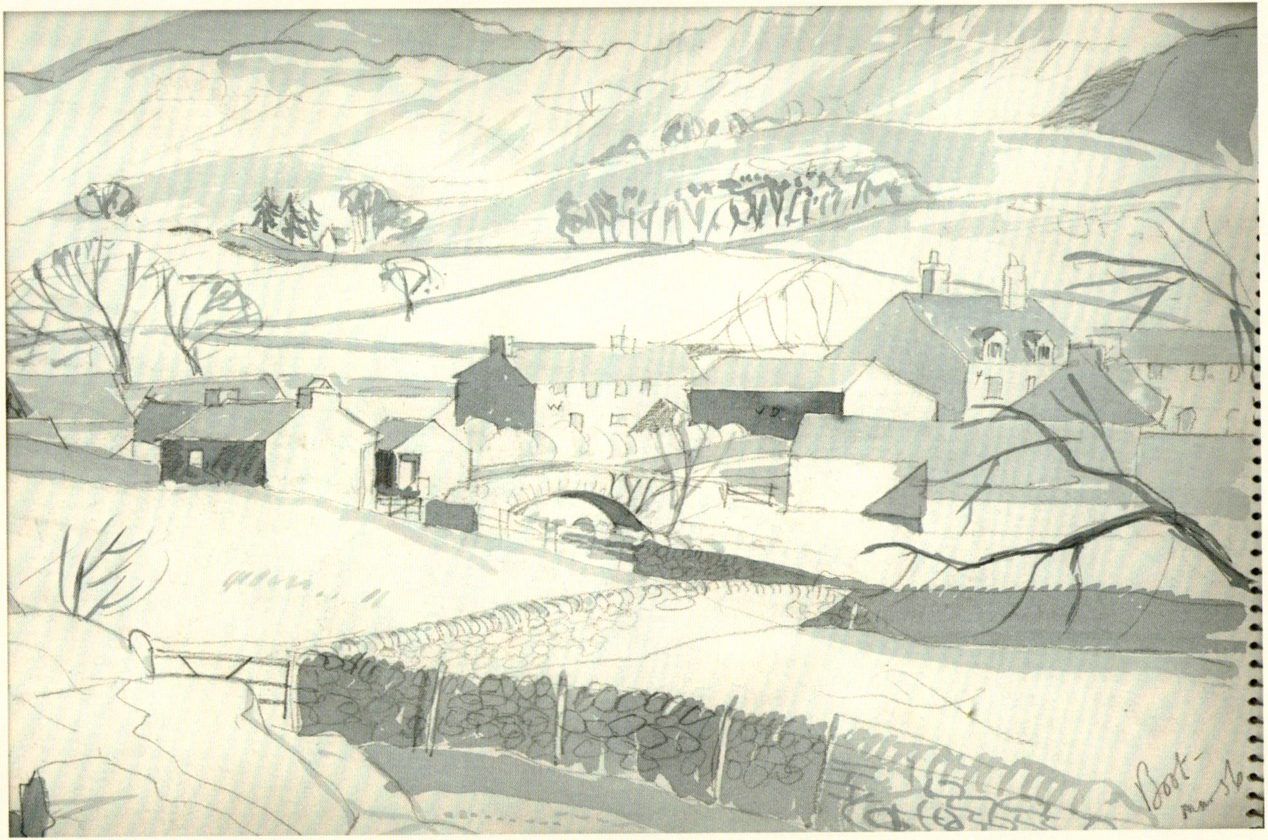

Boot, Eskdale; March 1956

1960 - 1961 Sketchbook

Charcoal Drawings

Between 1958 and 1961, Percy was drawing himself out of bouts of deep depression Many of the drawings are based on a long road disappearing into distant hills or settlements which he described as an allegory of life.

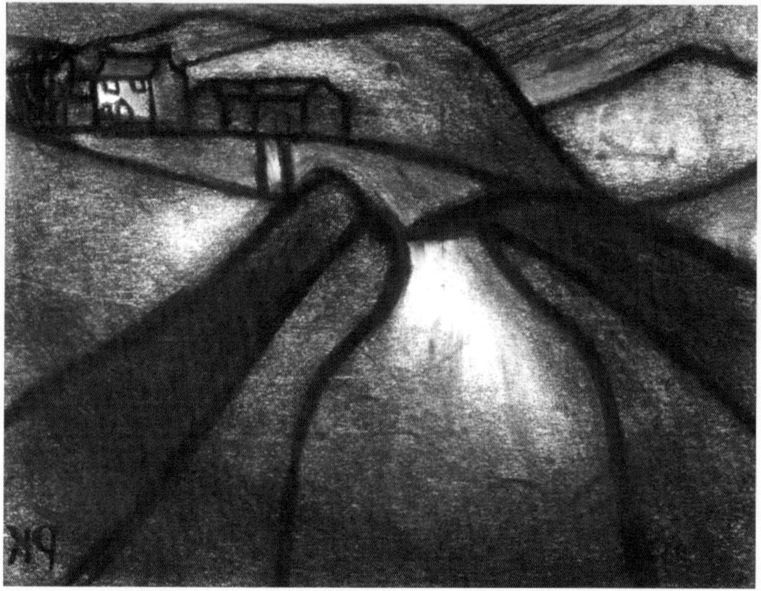

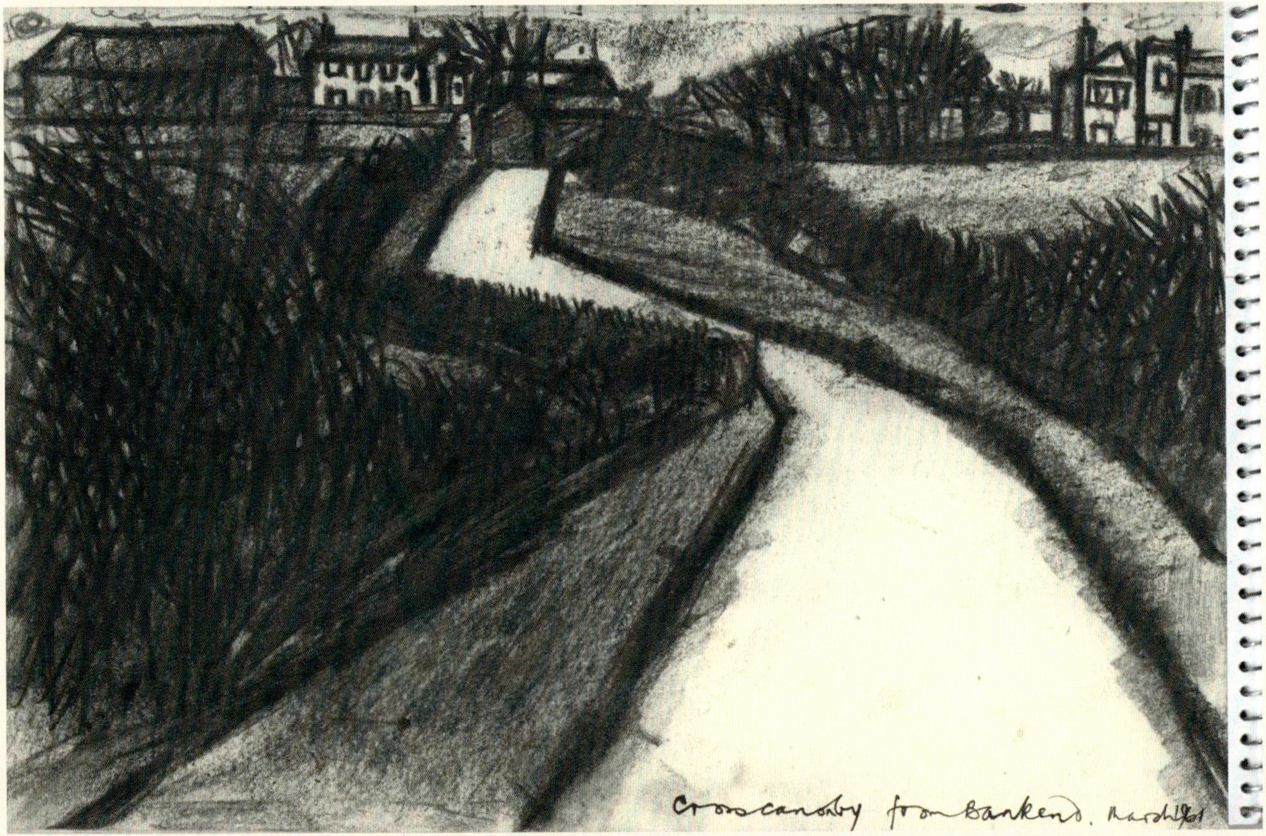

Crosscanonby from Bank End March 1961

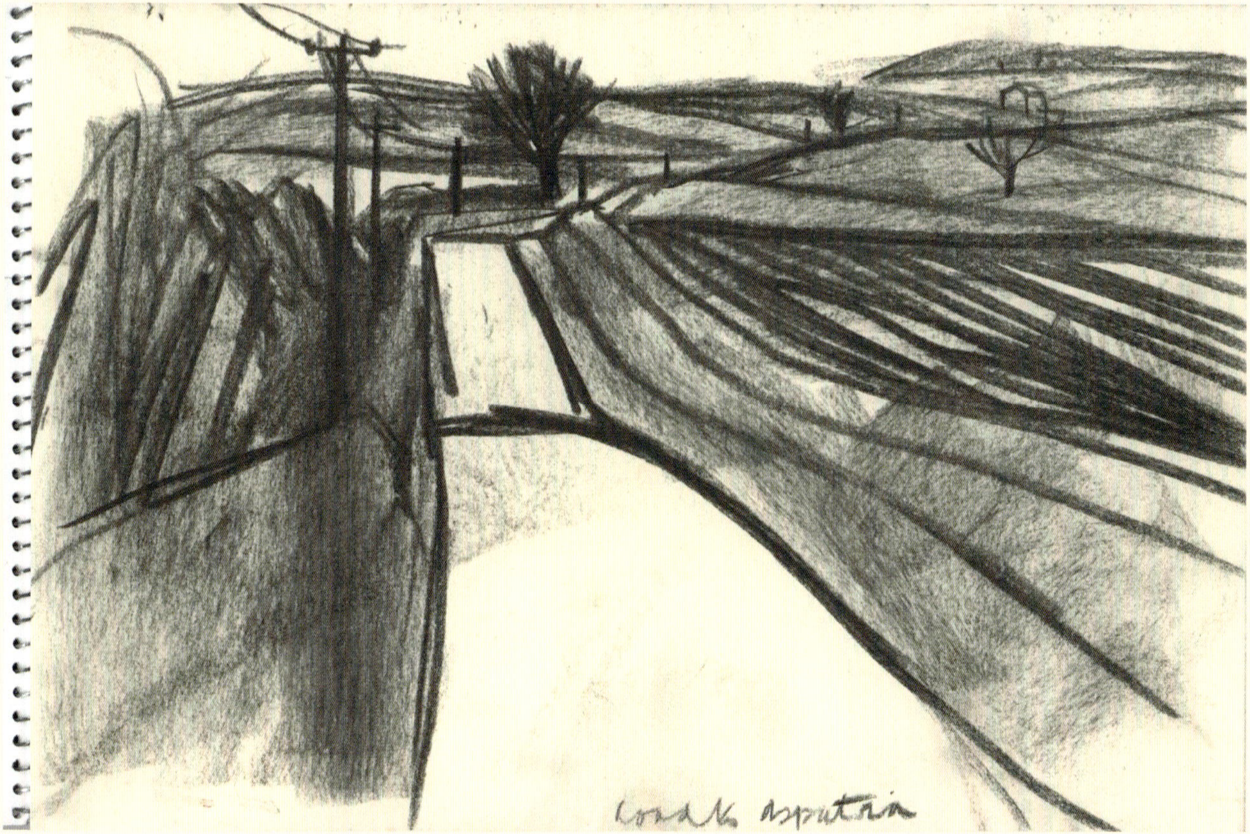

Road to Aspatria 1961

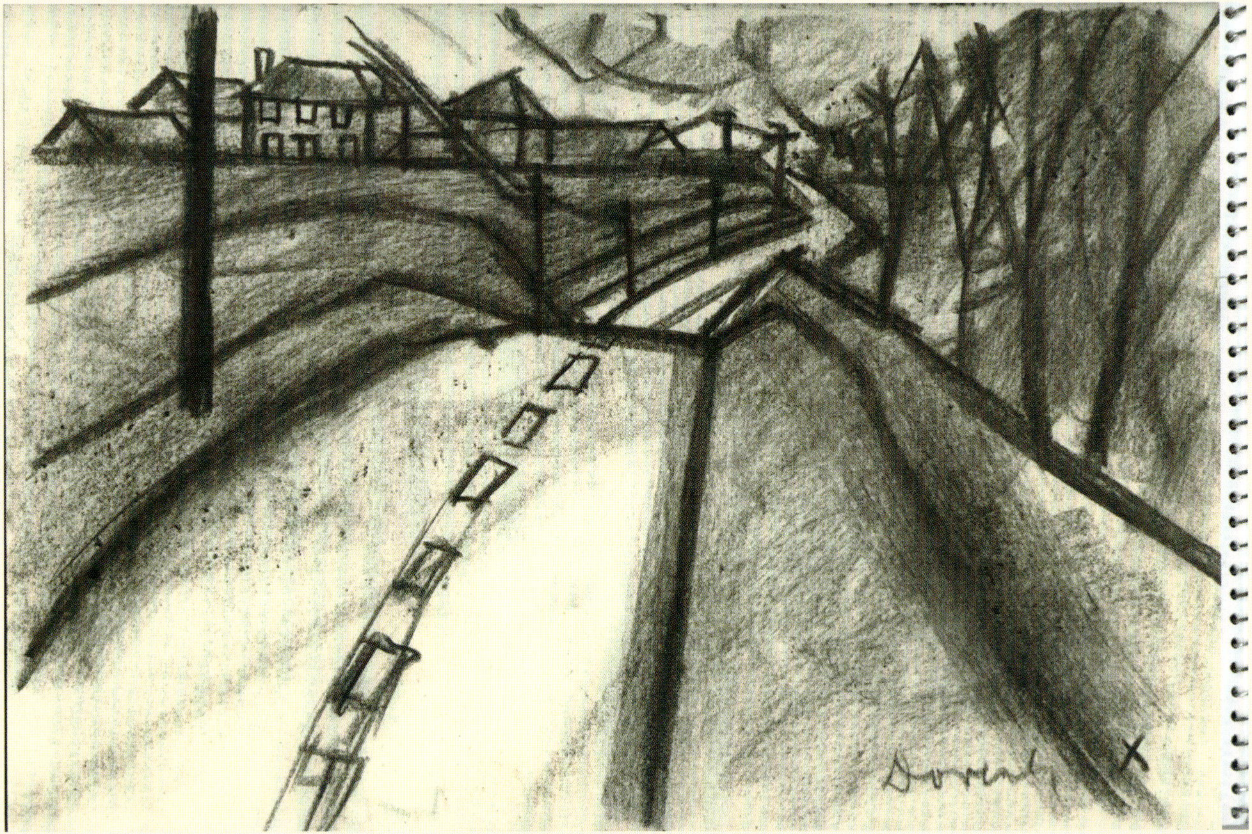

Dovenby March 1961

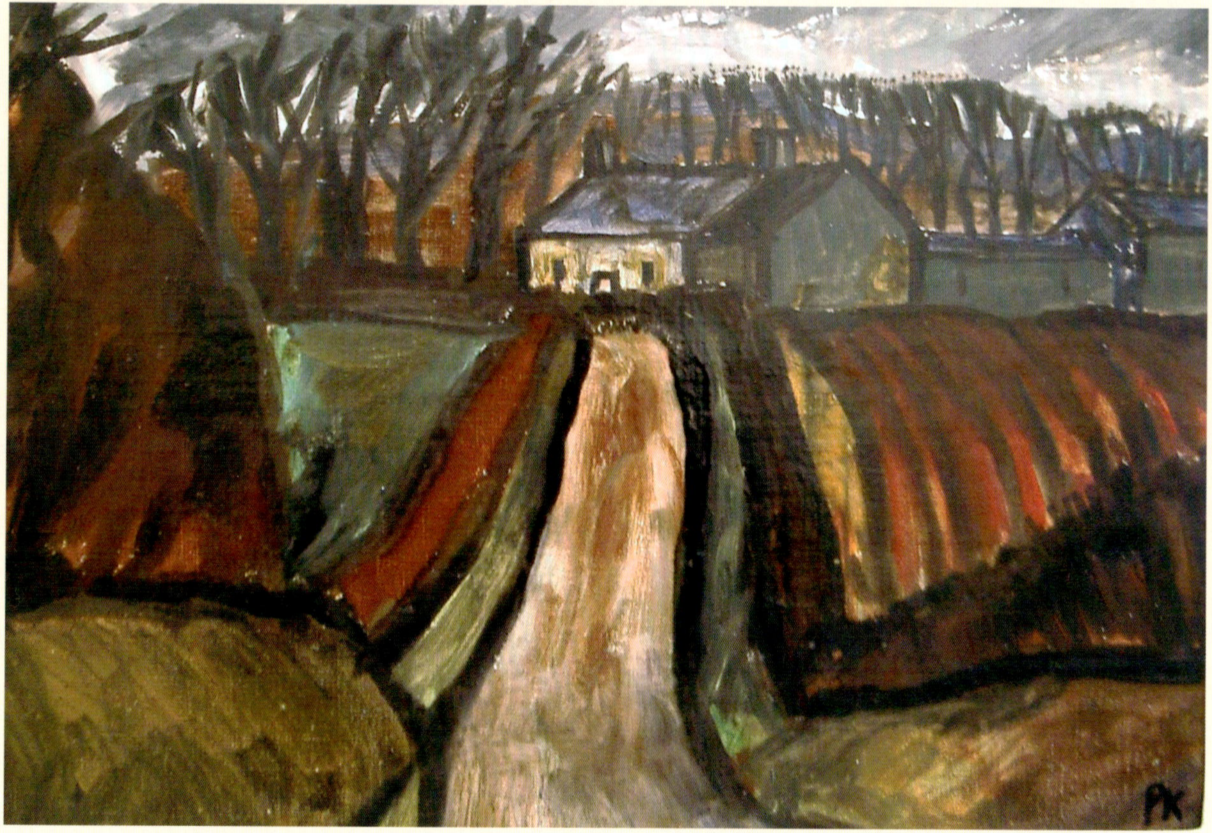

Road near Dovenby   Oil painting c 1965

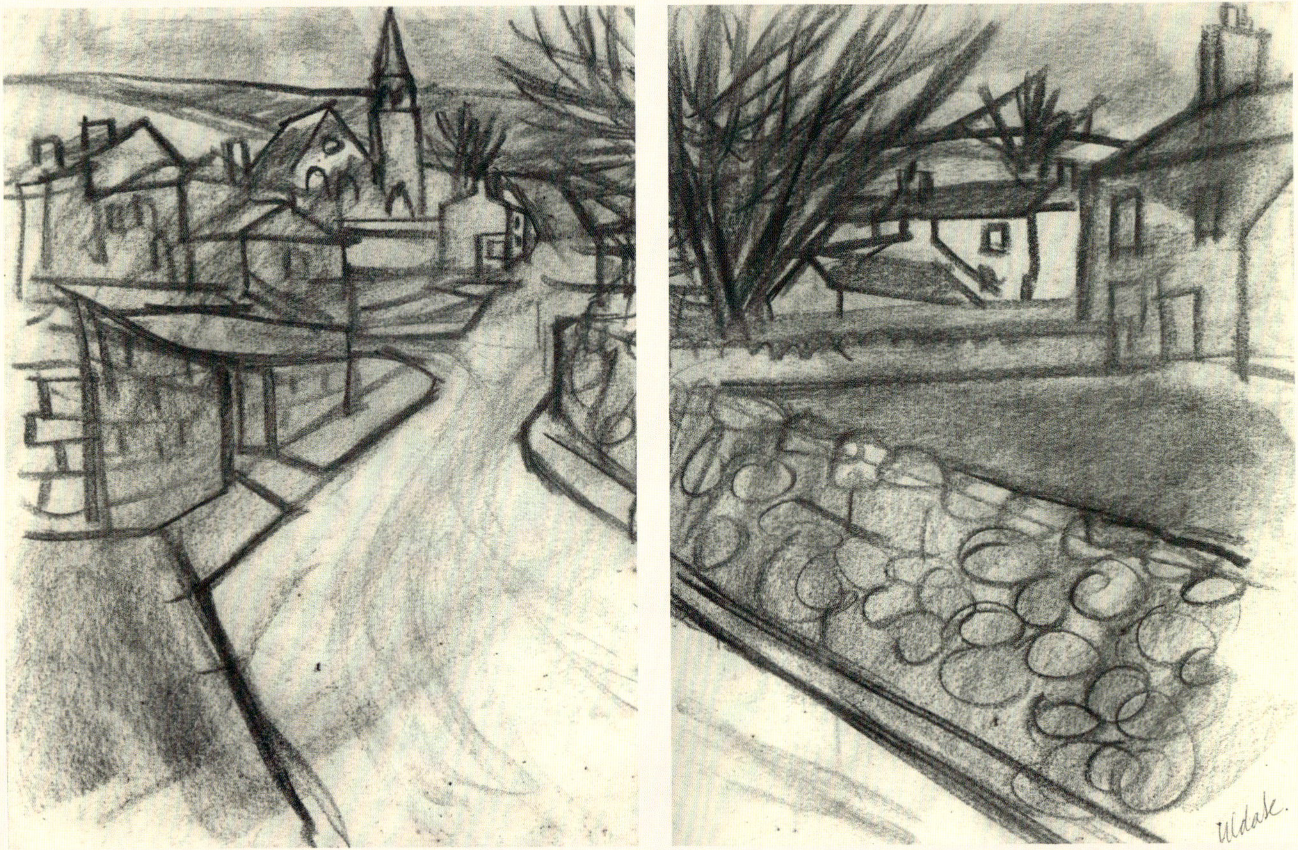

Sketch of Uldale 1958

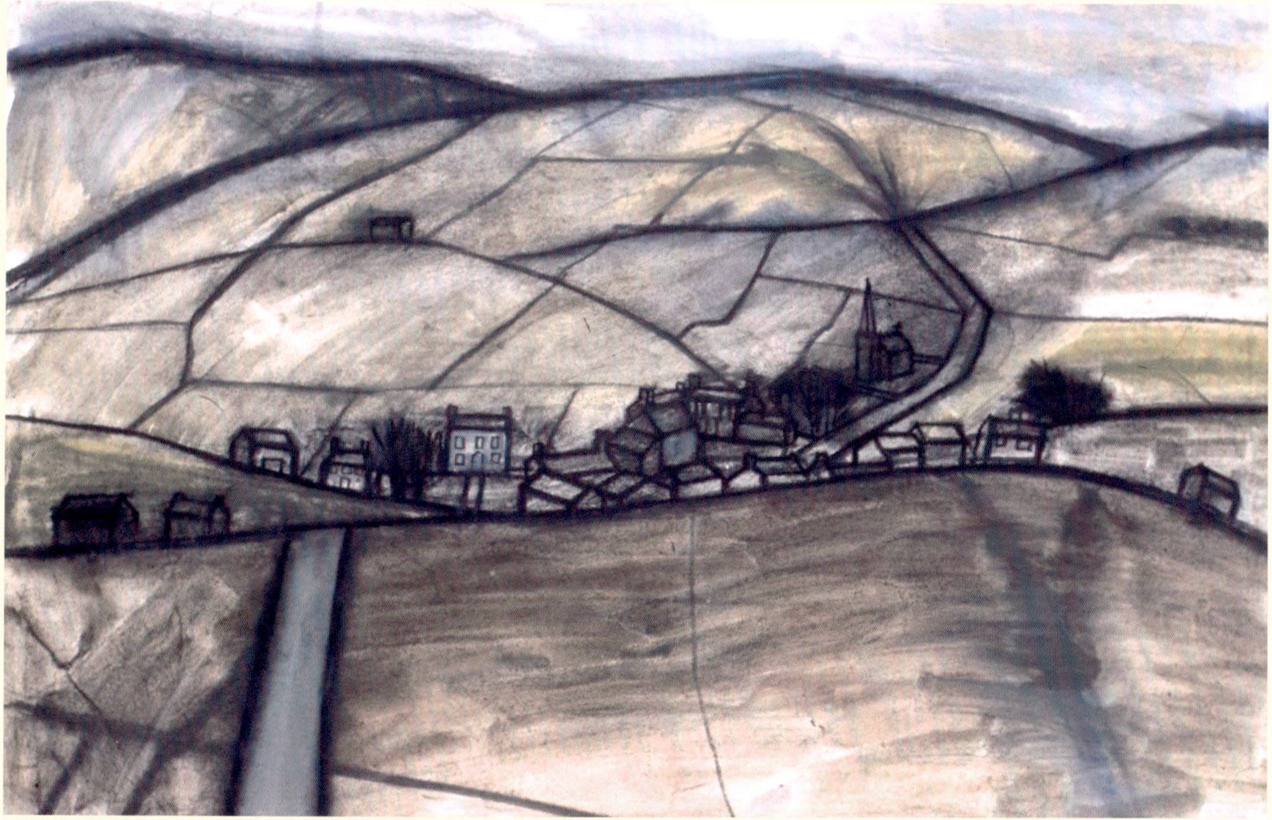

Charcoal drawing with watercolour of Uldale c 1962

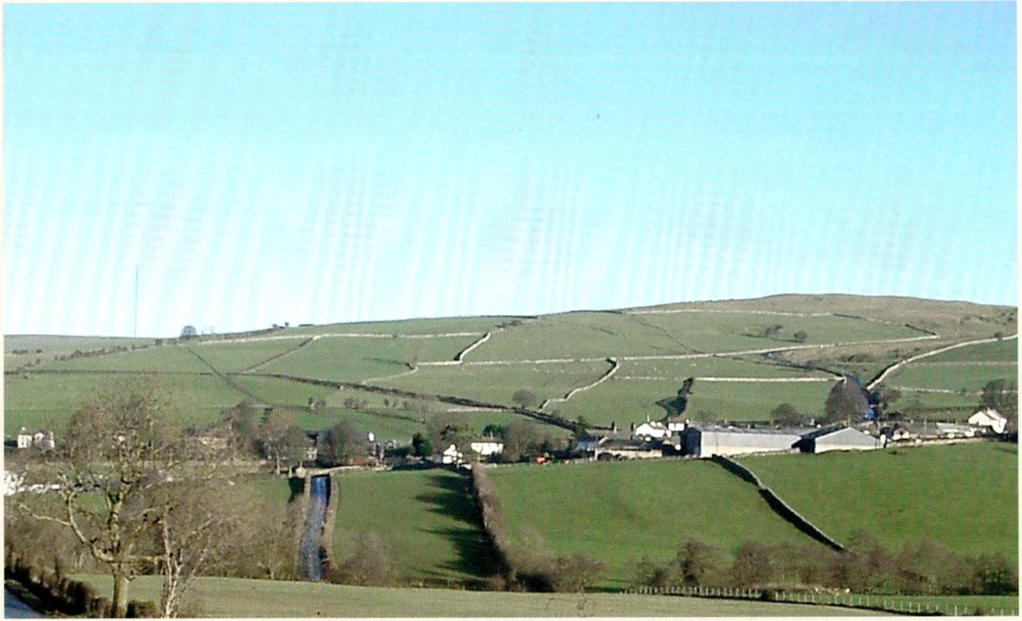

The drawing on the previous page was the cause of much discussion when shown in an exhibition at Castlegate House in 1996. Its location was disputed because Uldale has no church. It was then discovered that Uldale did have a church which was dramatically demolished in September 1963 when repairs to the underpinning were considered too expensive. The site is now a children's playground. The 1956 sketch confirms this story. The above photograph was taken December 2006.

COLLEGE DAYS

Carlisle College of Art and Design

1961 - 1965

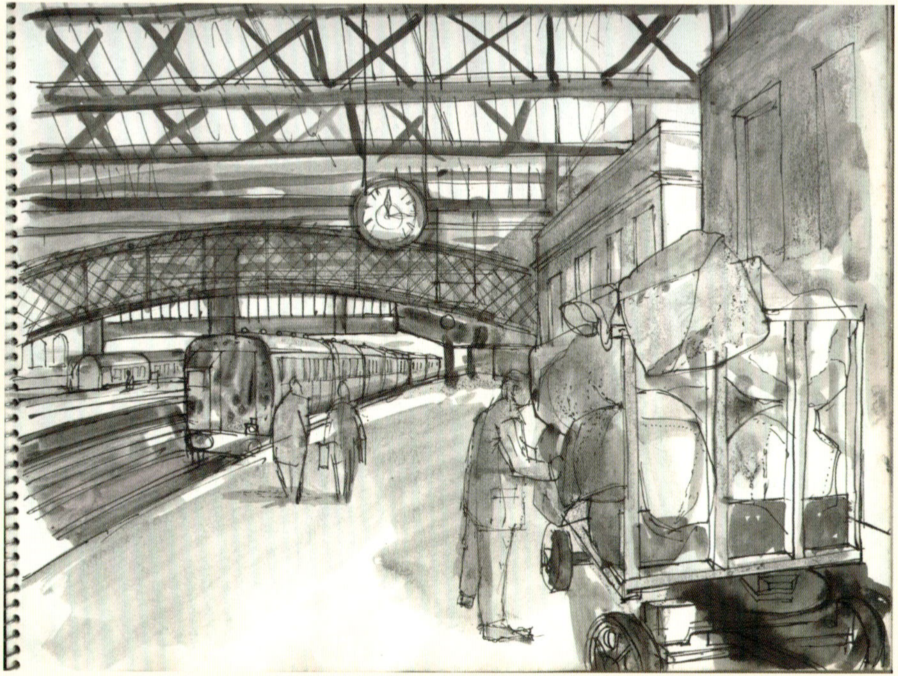

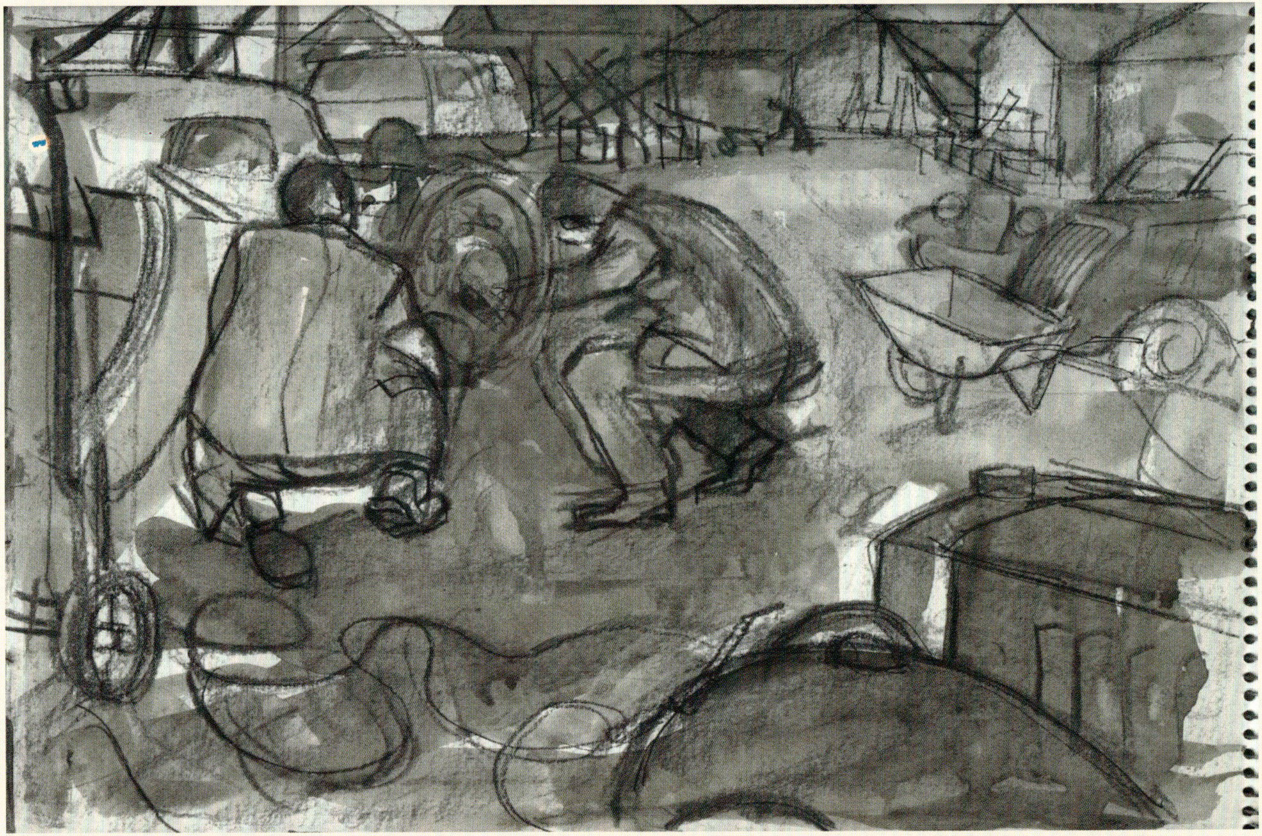

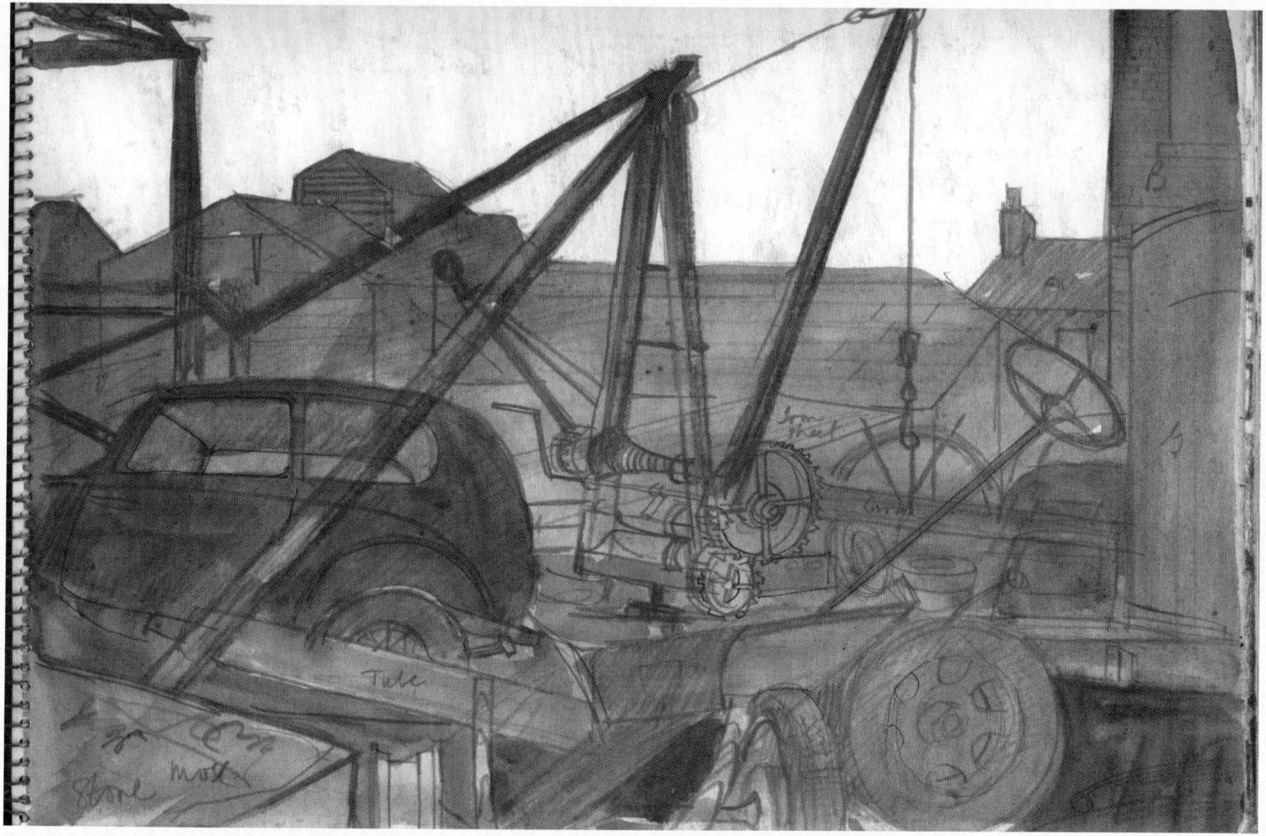

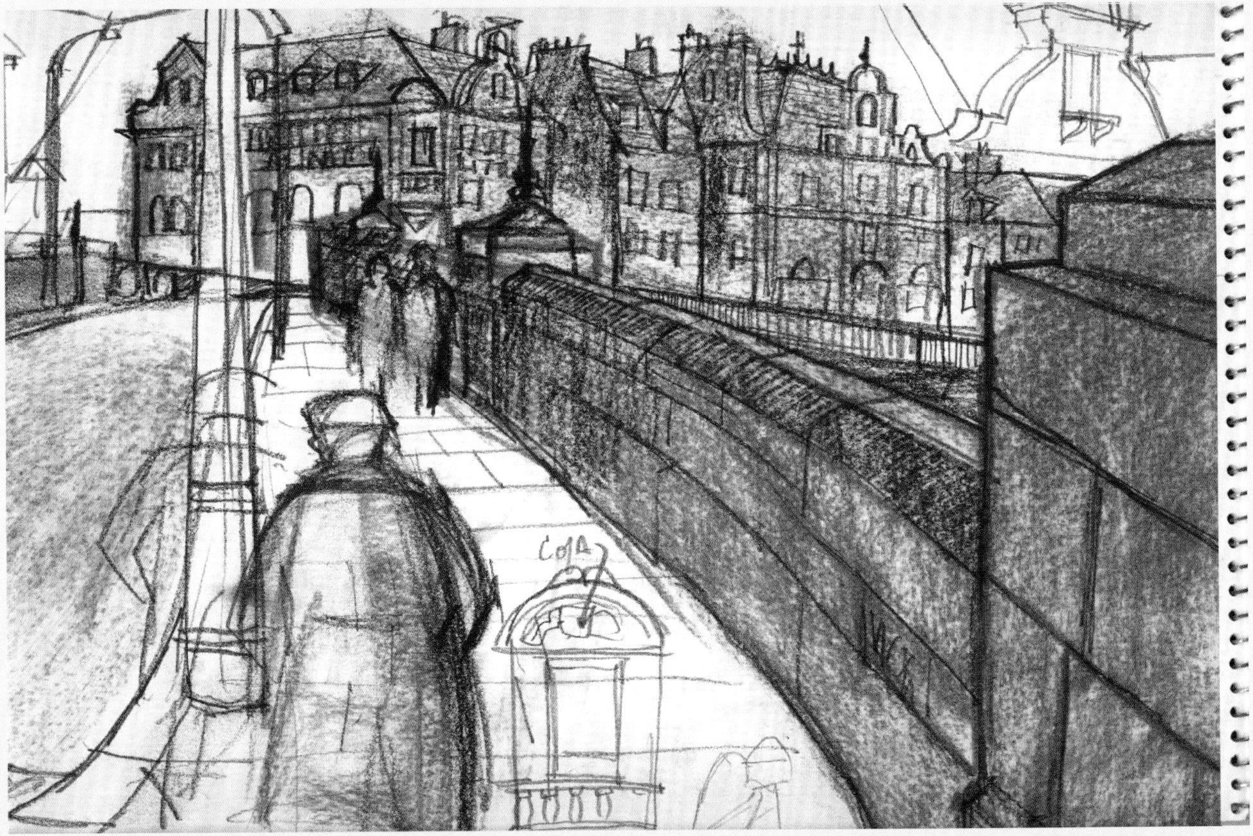

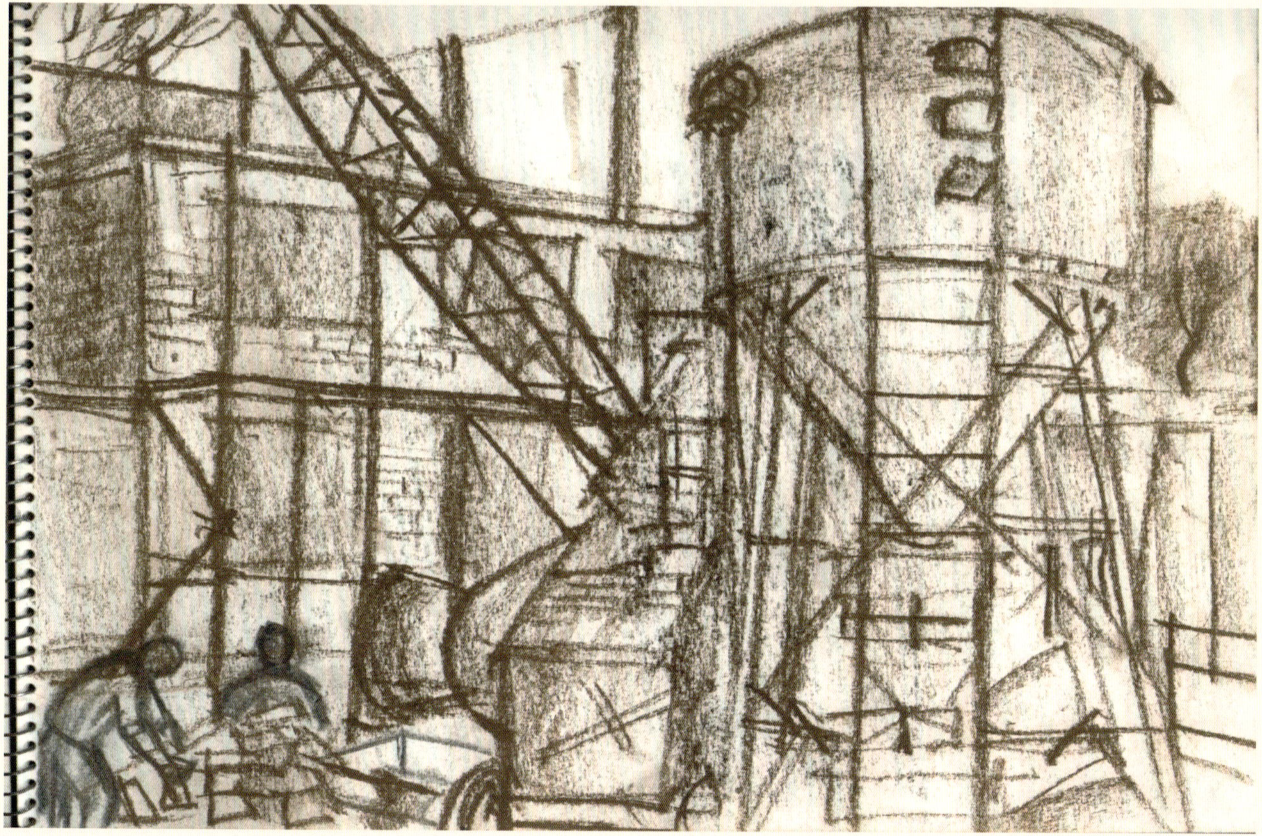

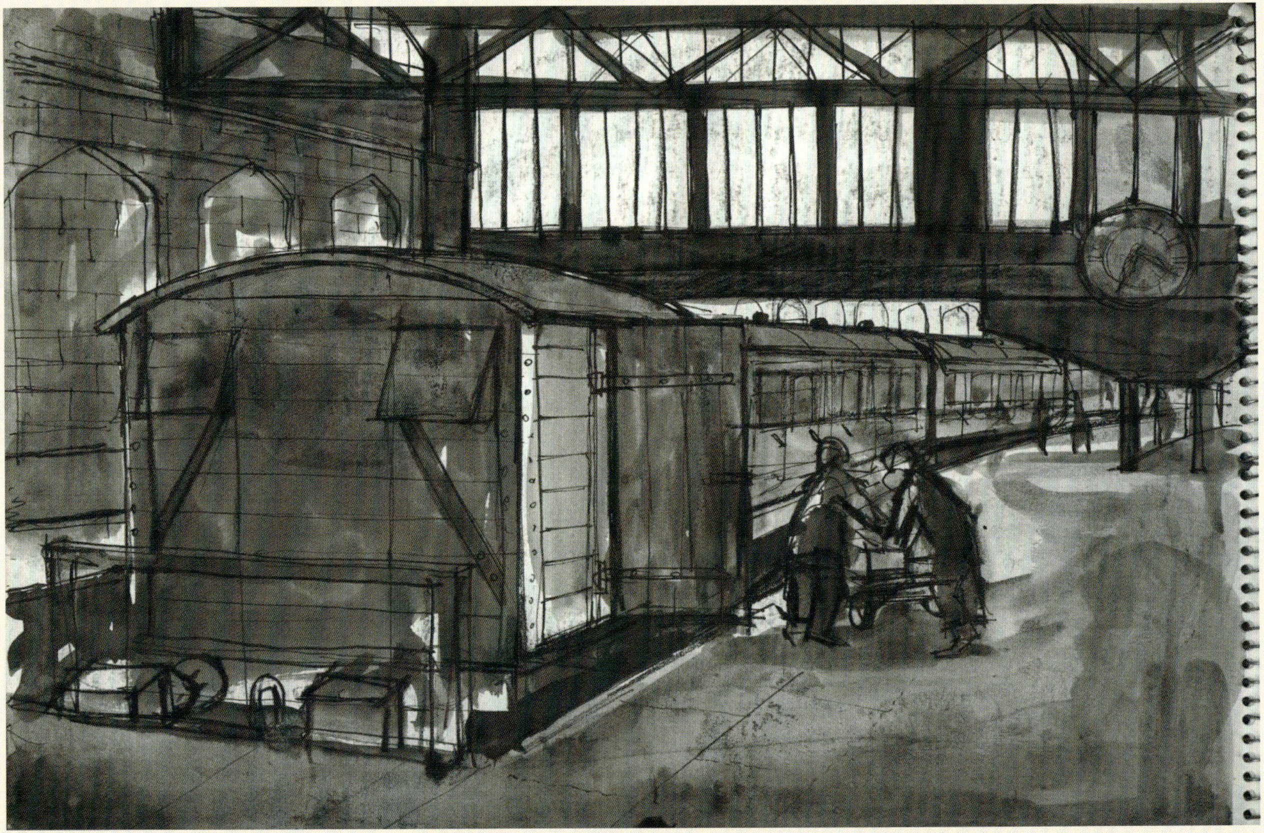

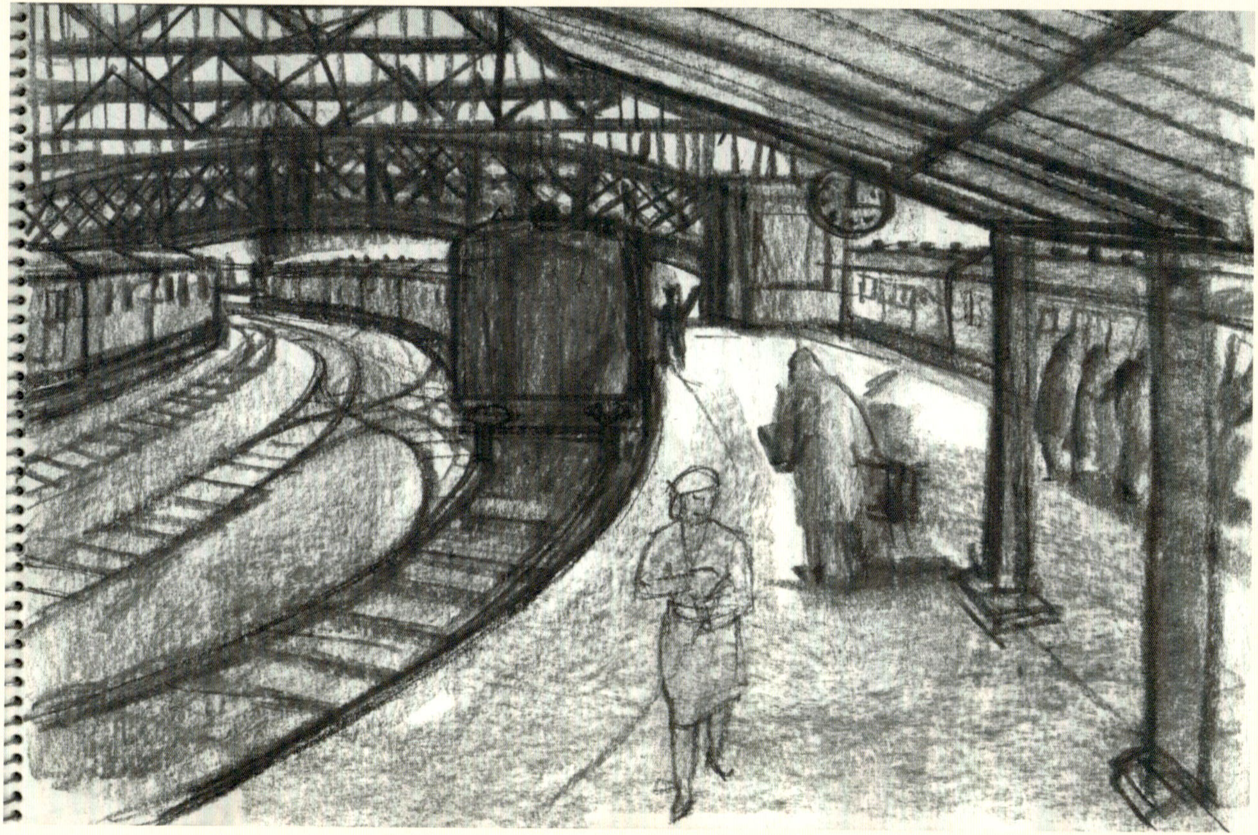

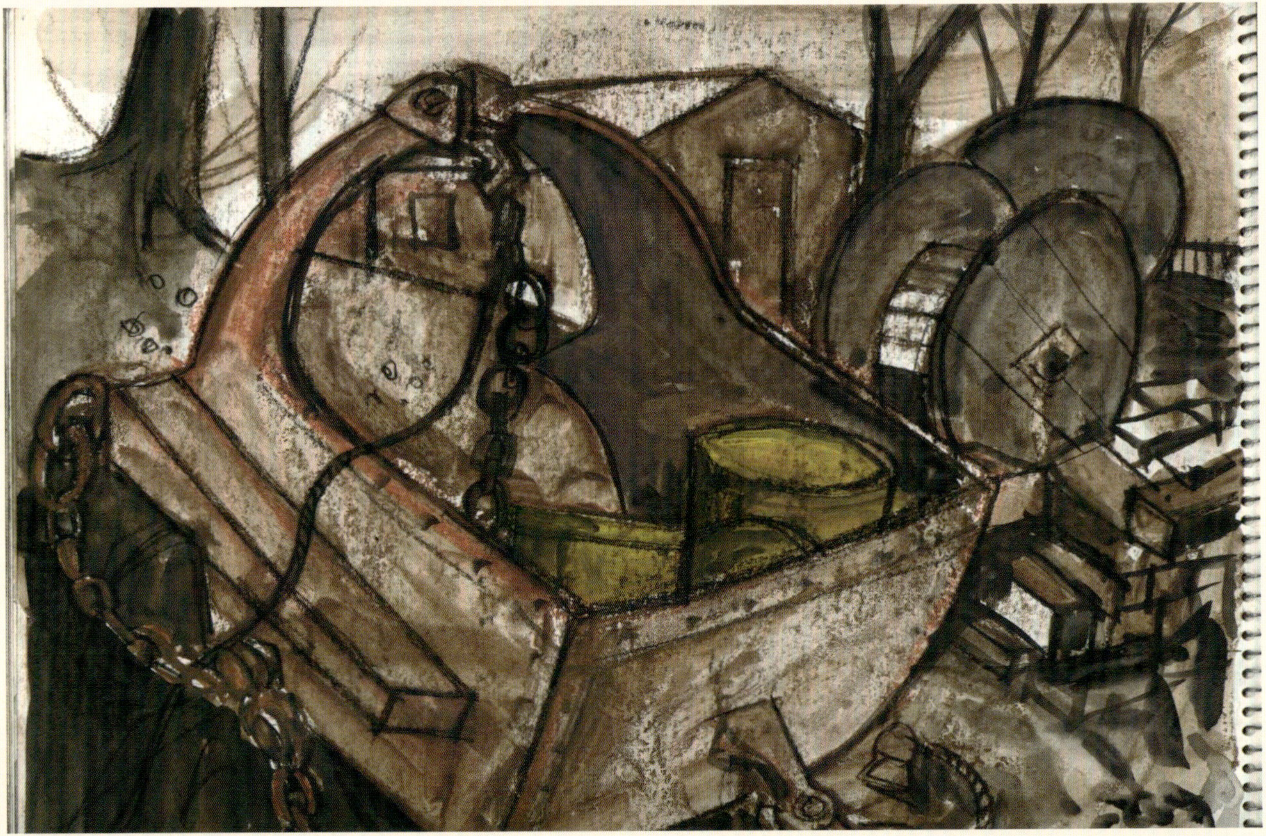

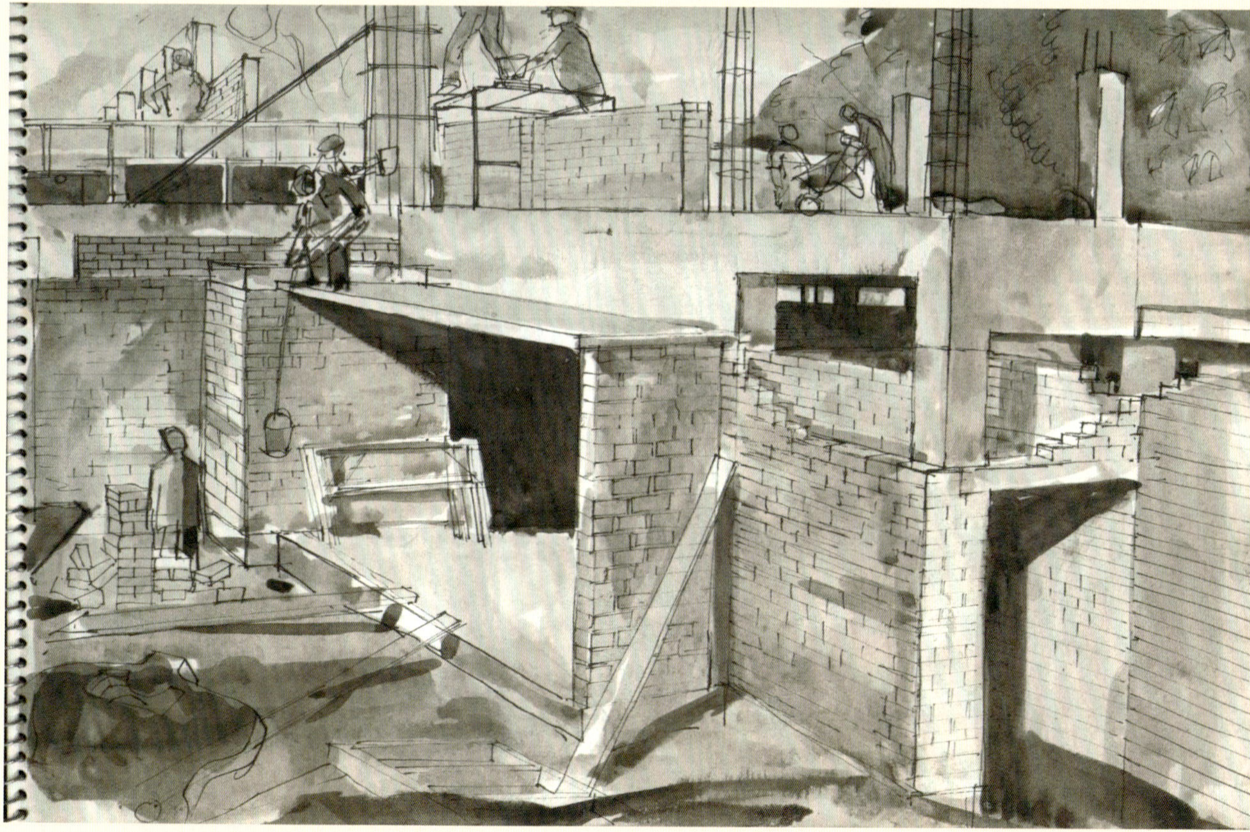

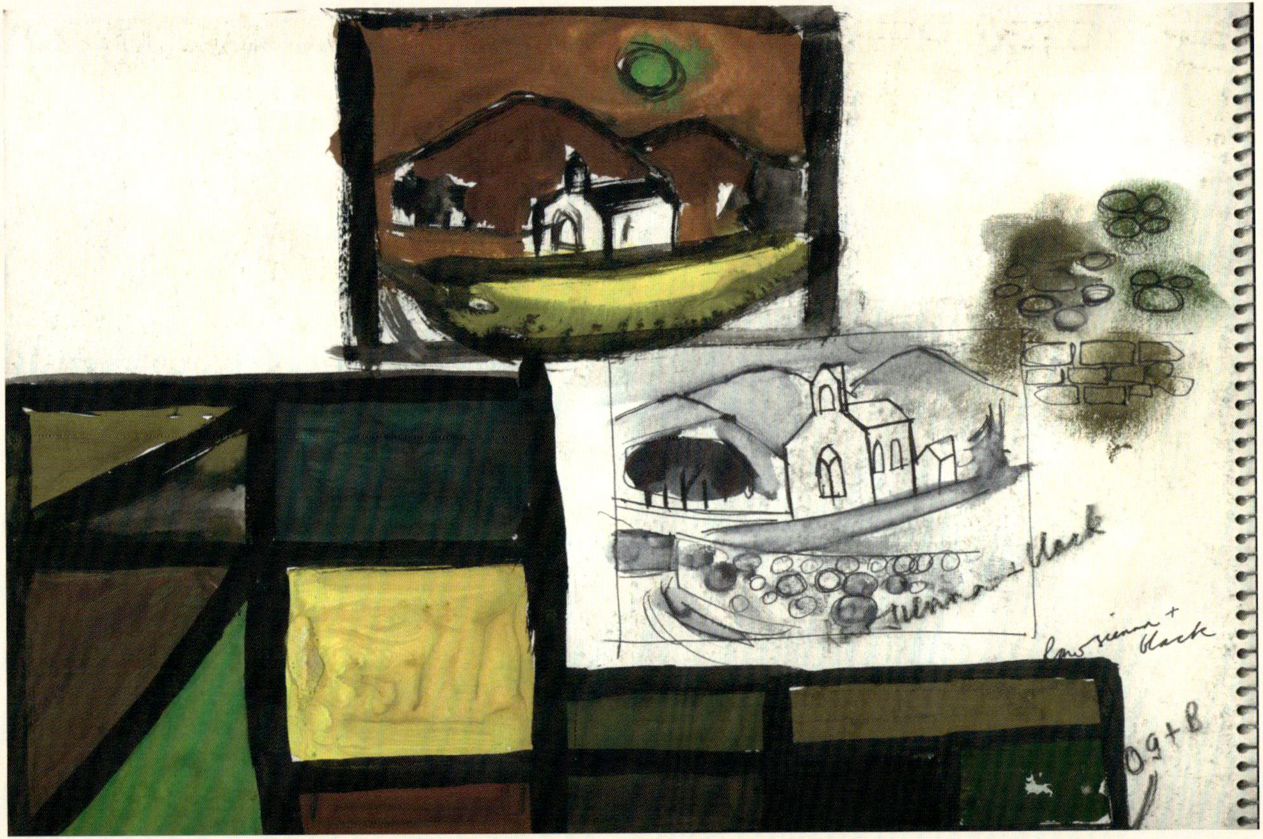
Raw sienna + black
Og + B

CORNWALL

From the mid 1950s, Percy Kelly would go to Cornwall each year in the summer as a tutor in a painting summer school in St Ives run by Charles Breaker. From the sketch books we find that he spent a lot of his spare time exploring the area around St Ives.

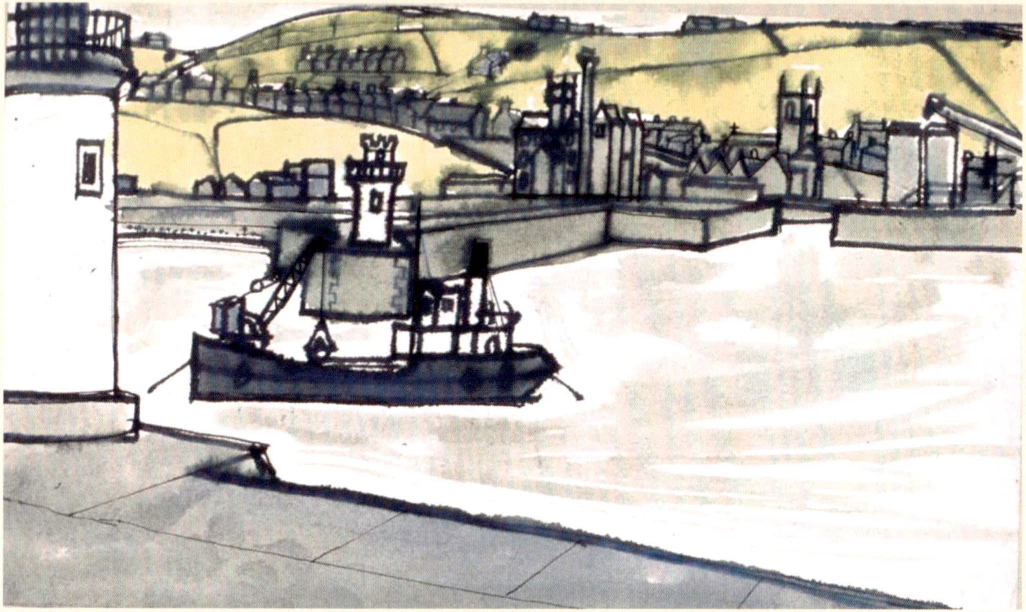

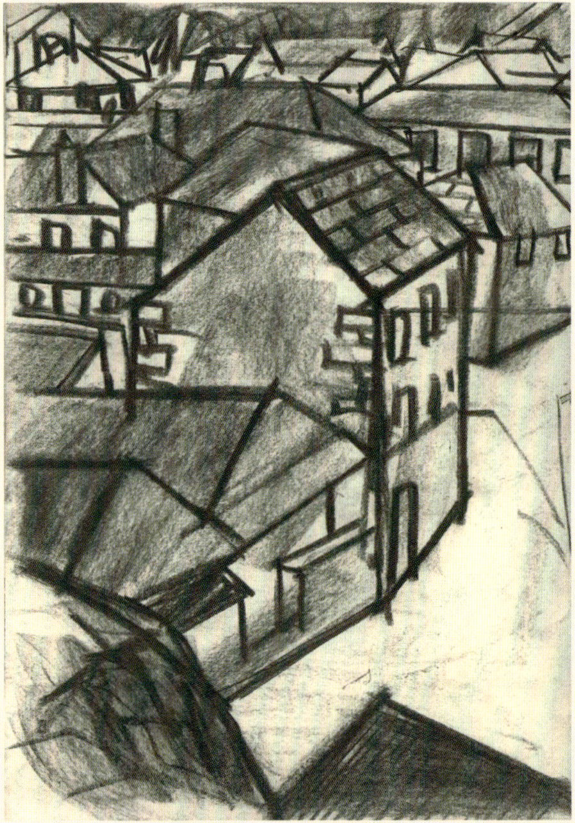

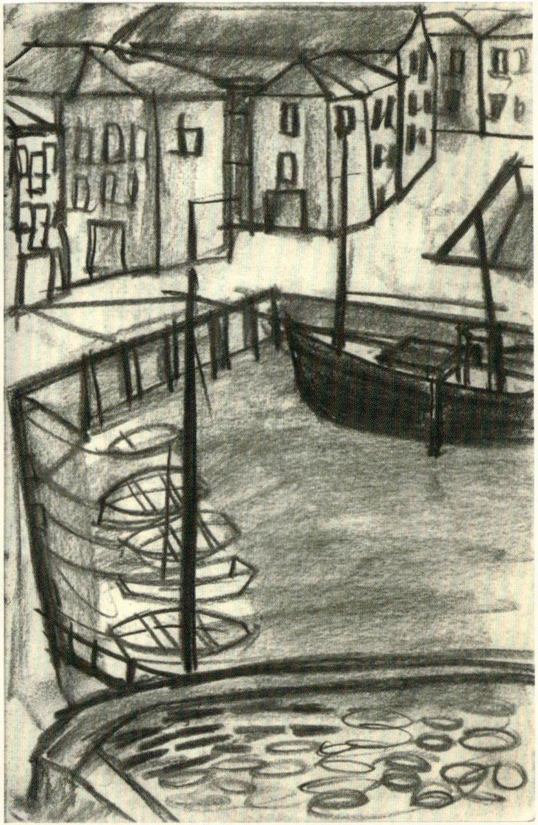

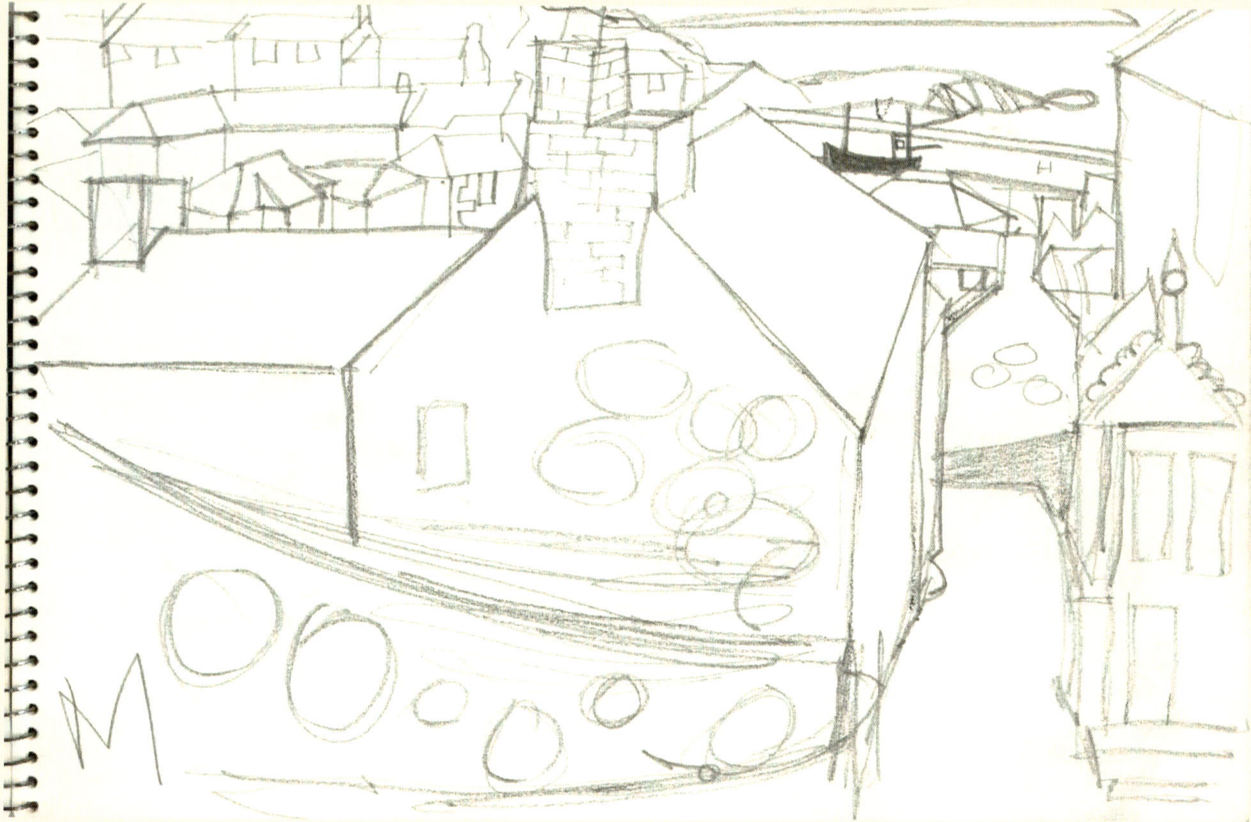

Mousehole

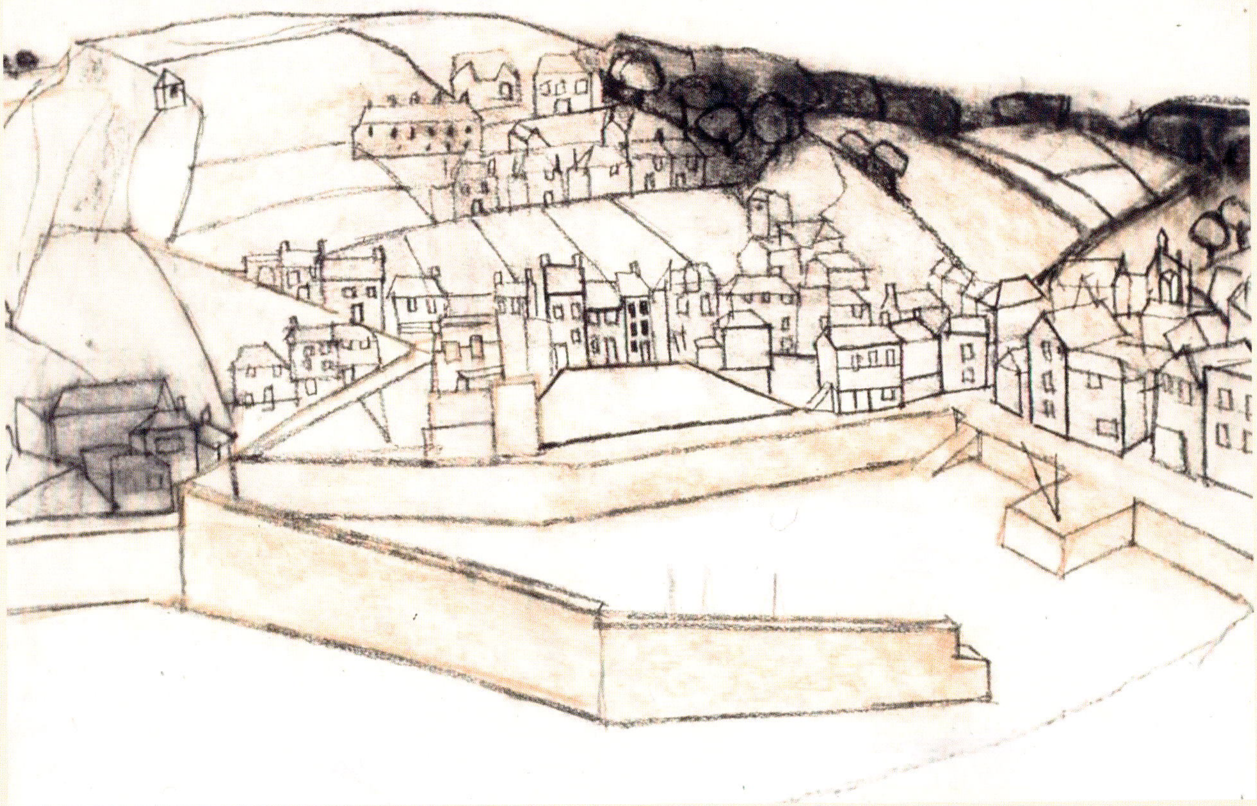

Mousehole

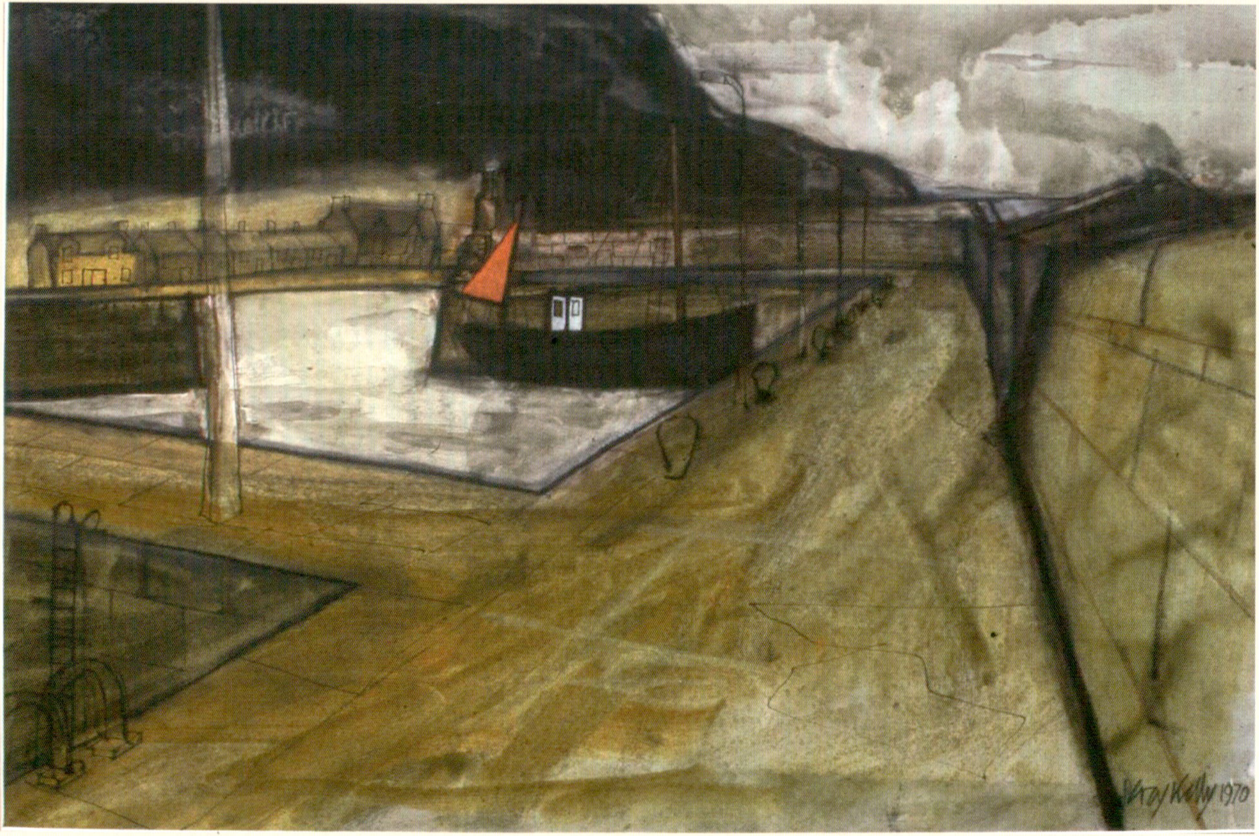

Mousehole painting

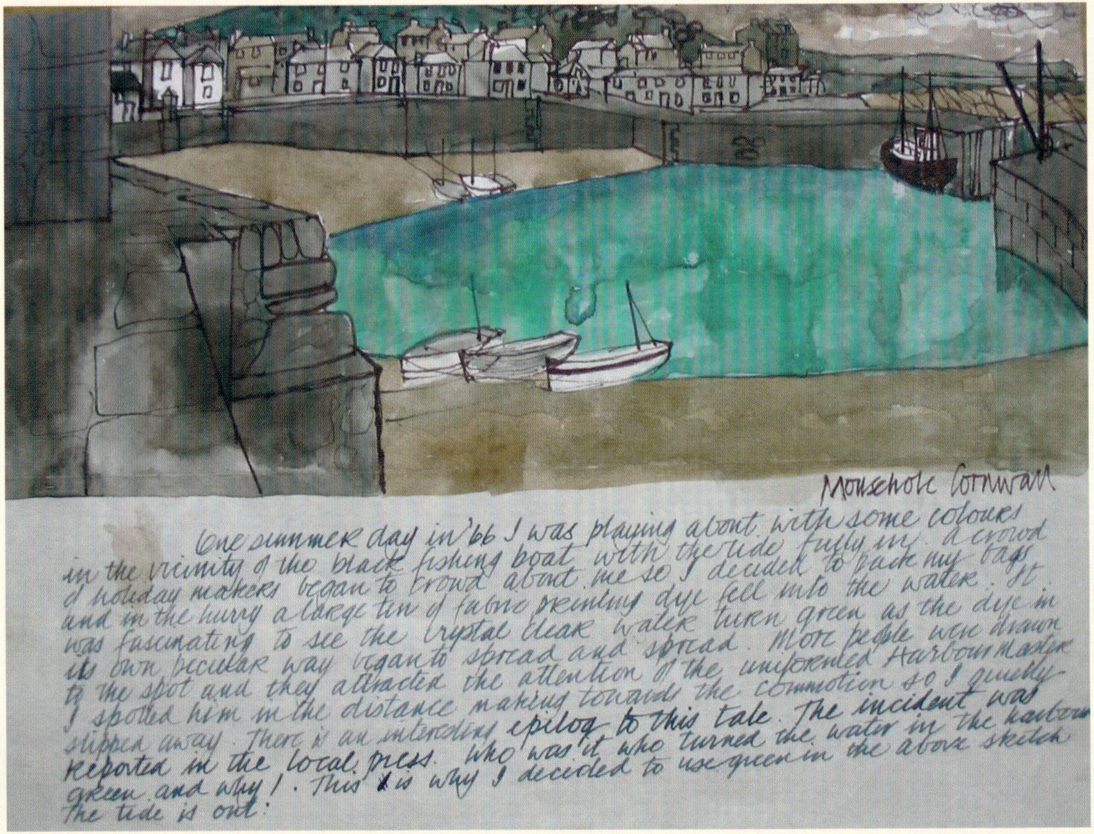

One summer day in '66 I was playing about with some colours in the vicinity of the black fishing boat with the tide fully in. A crowd of holiday makers began to crowd about me so I decided to pack my bags and in the hurry a large tin of fabric printing dye fell into the water. It was fascinating to see the crystal clear water turn green as the dye in its own peculiar way began to spread and spread. More people were drawn to the spot and they attracted the attention of the uniformed Harbour Master. I spotted him in the distance making towards the commotion so I quickly slipped away. There is an interesting epilog to this tale. The incident was reported in the local press. Who was it who turned the water in the harbour green and why! This is why I decided to use green in the above sketch. The tide is out!

Letter to Joan David

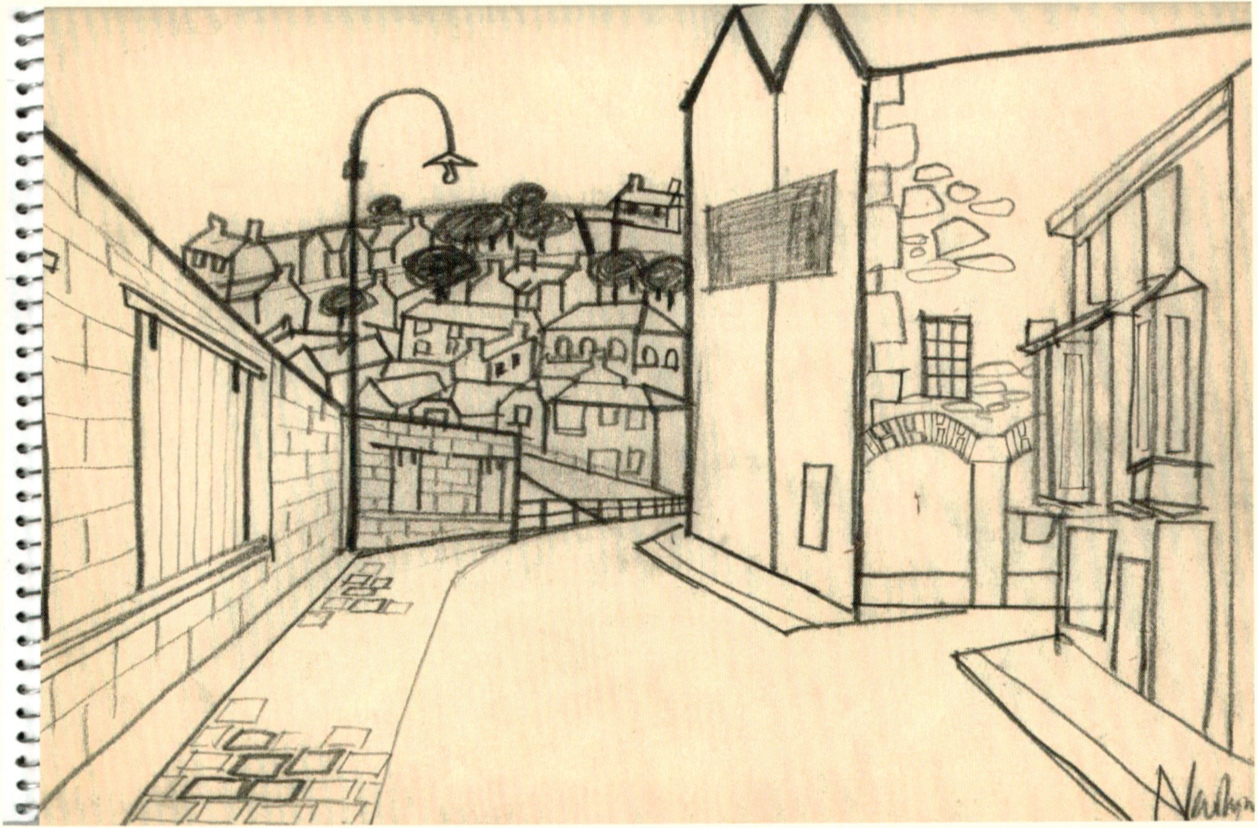

Newlyn 1966

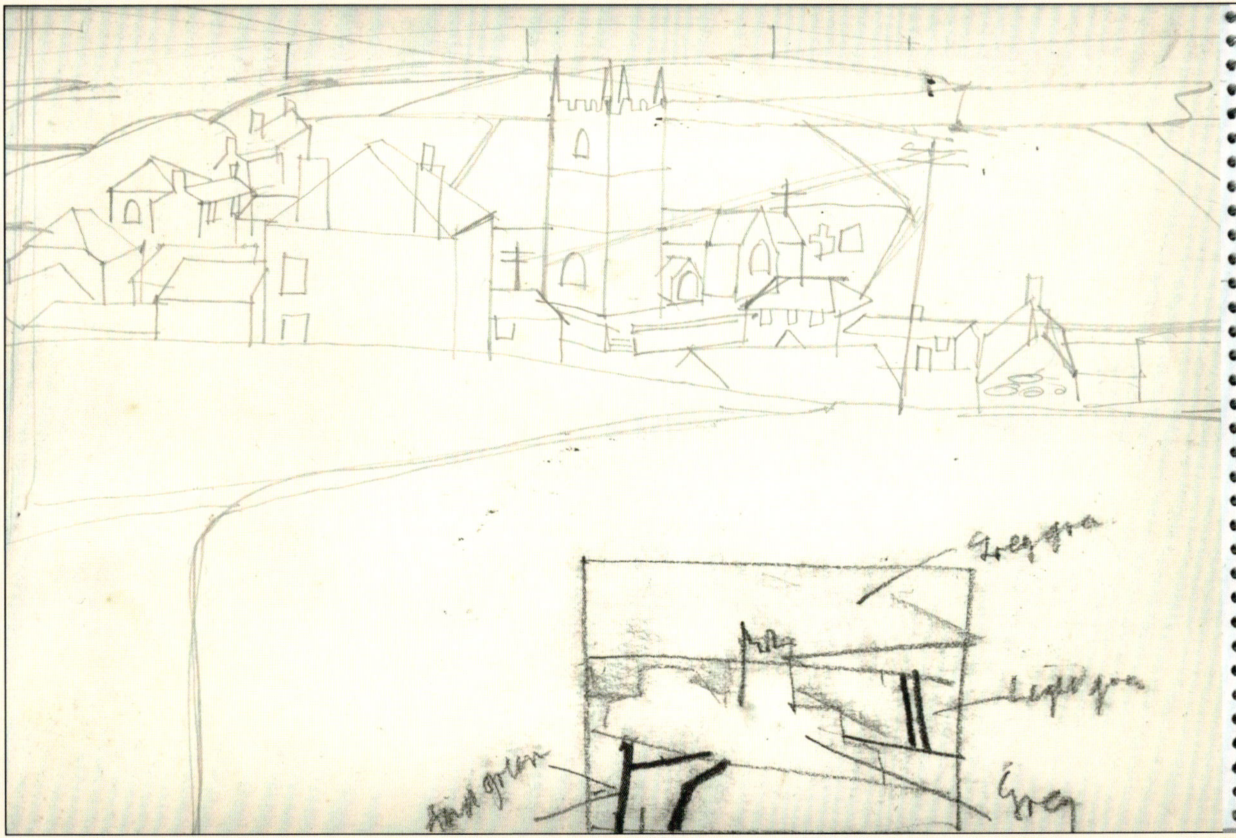

Zennor sketch

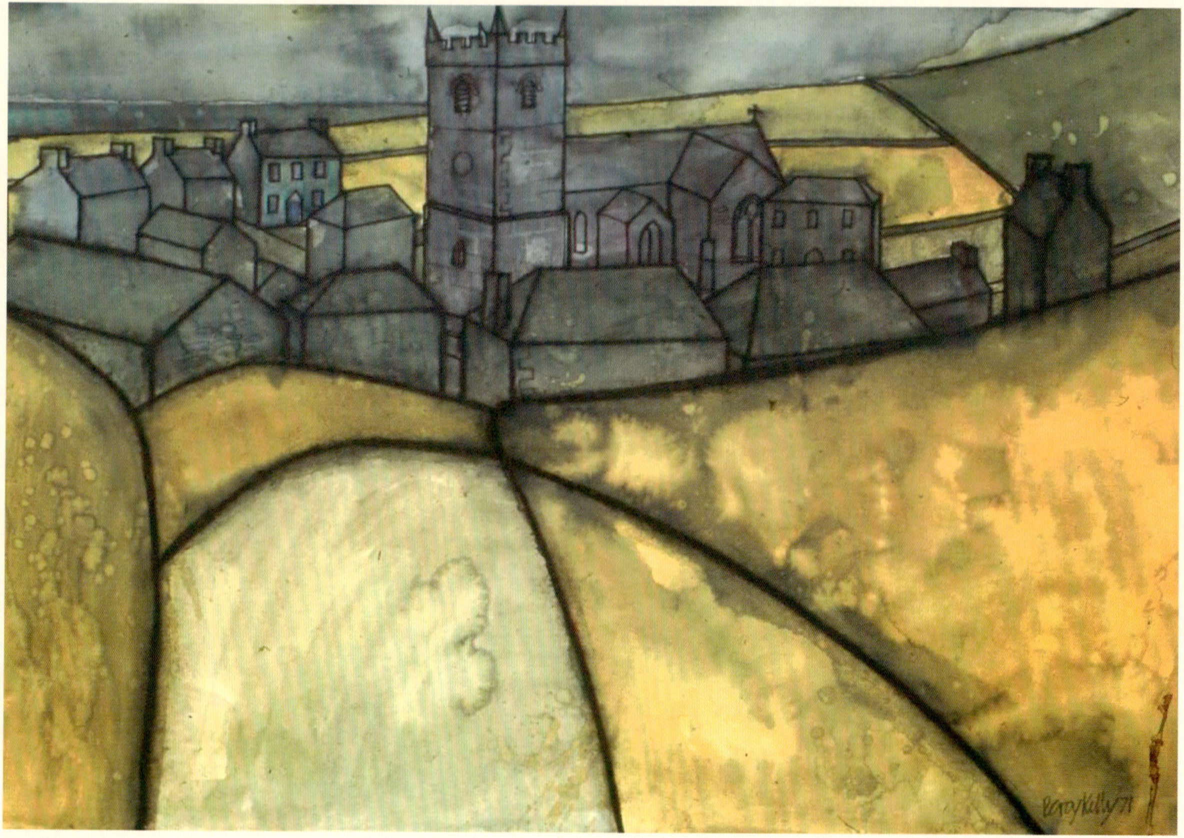

Zennor 1971 Watercolour/inkpainting

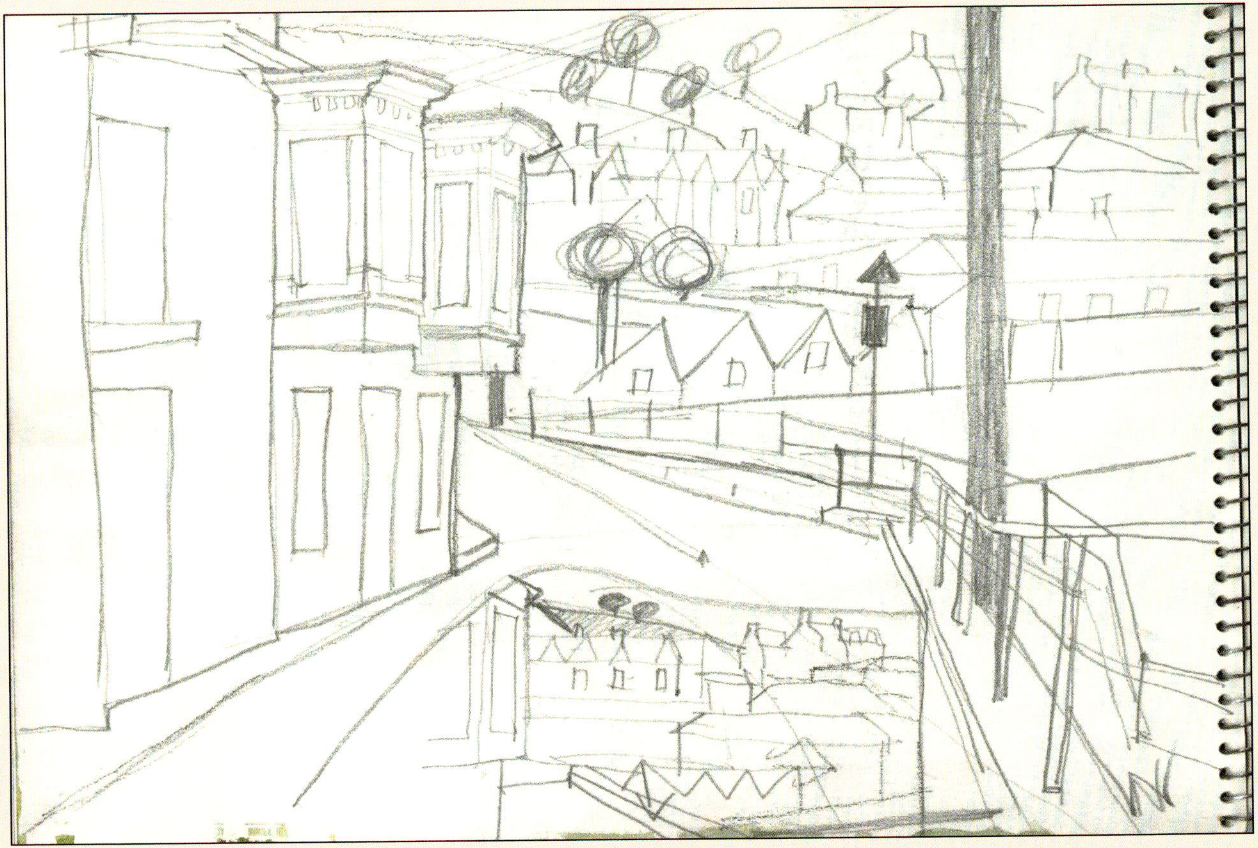

Newlyn

SMALL SKETCHBOOK 1962

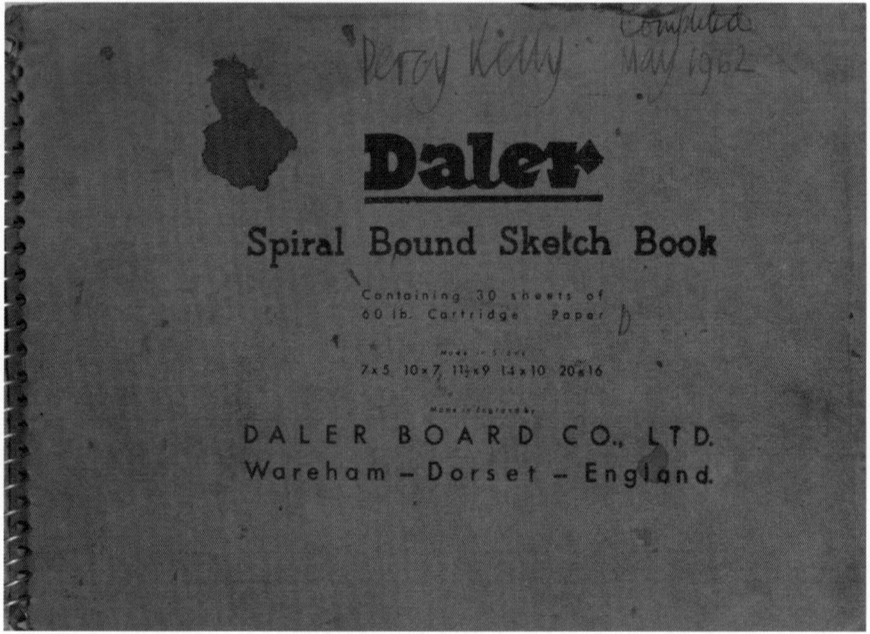

A small pocket (7" x 5") sketchbook completed 1962 containing 38 drawings and painting sketches. Some of these were referred to in later large paintings and drawings

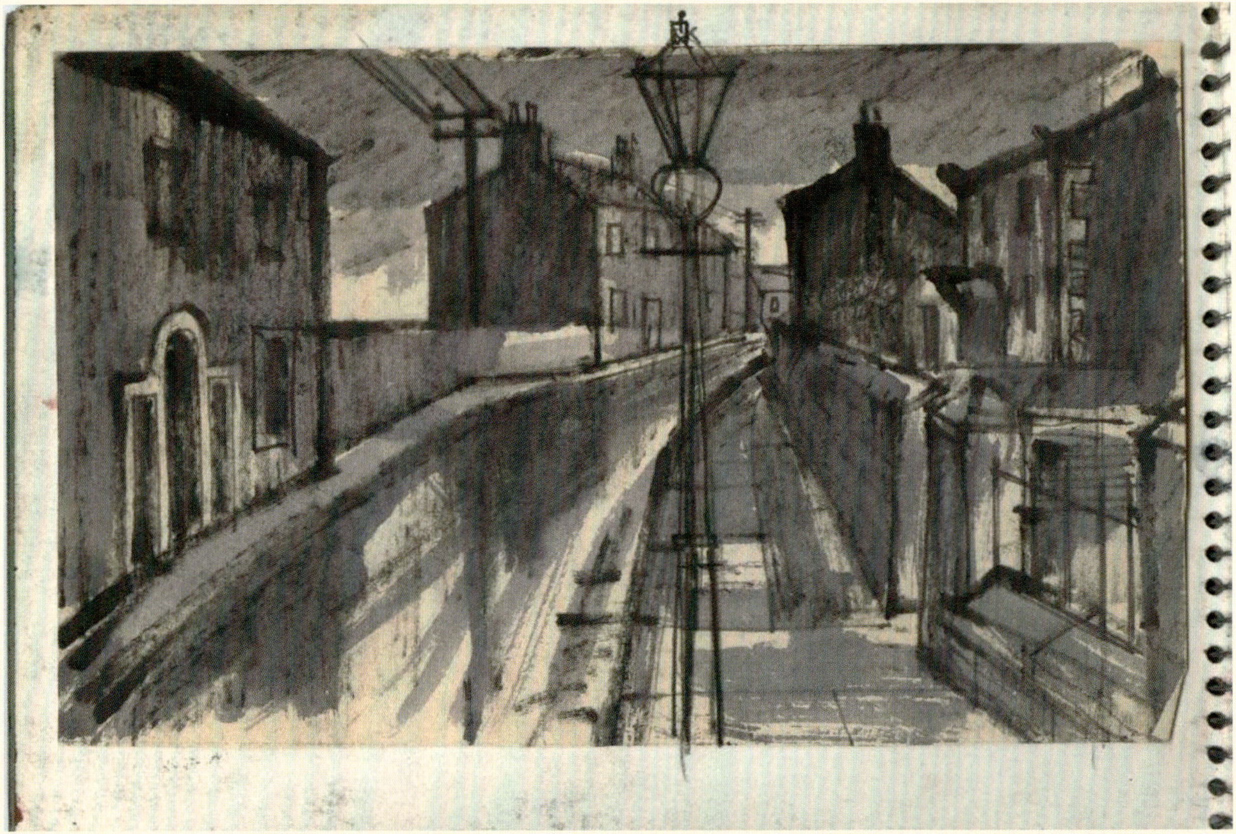

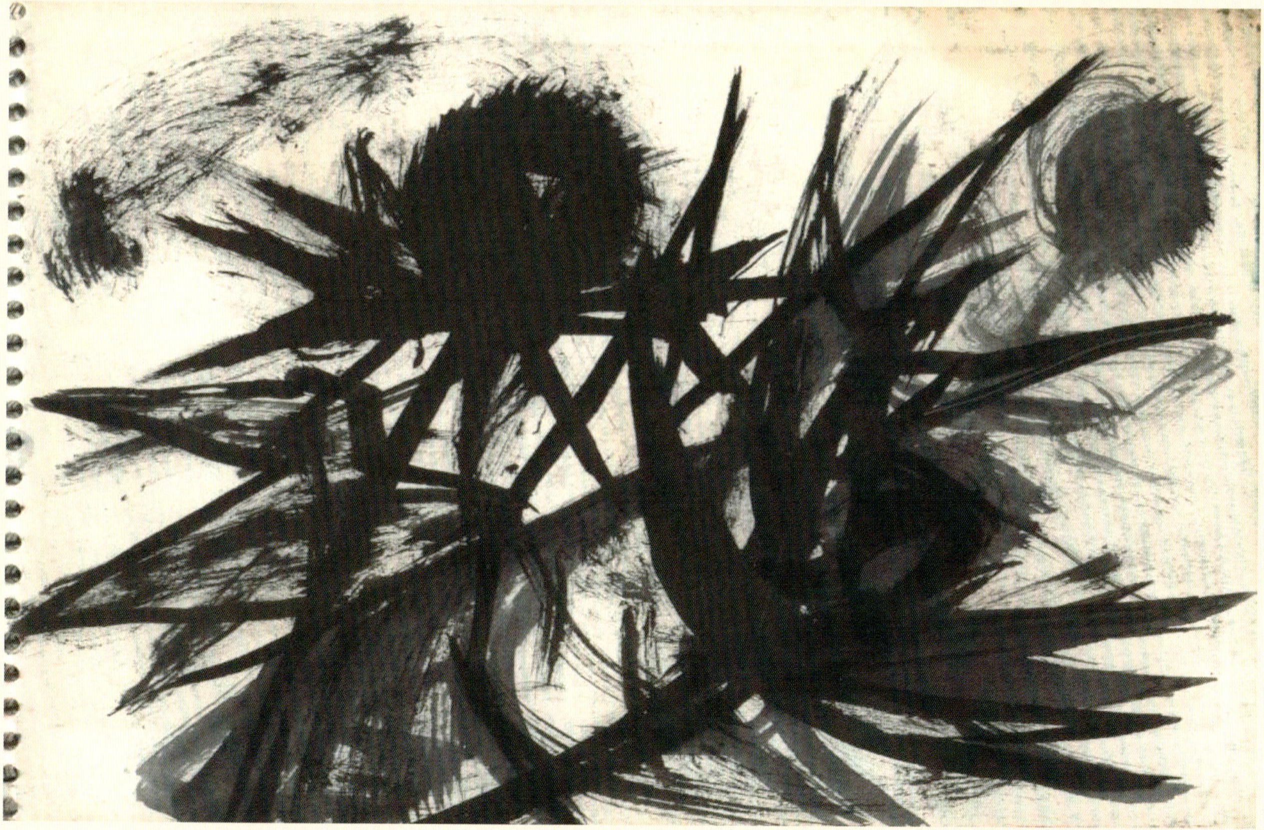

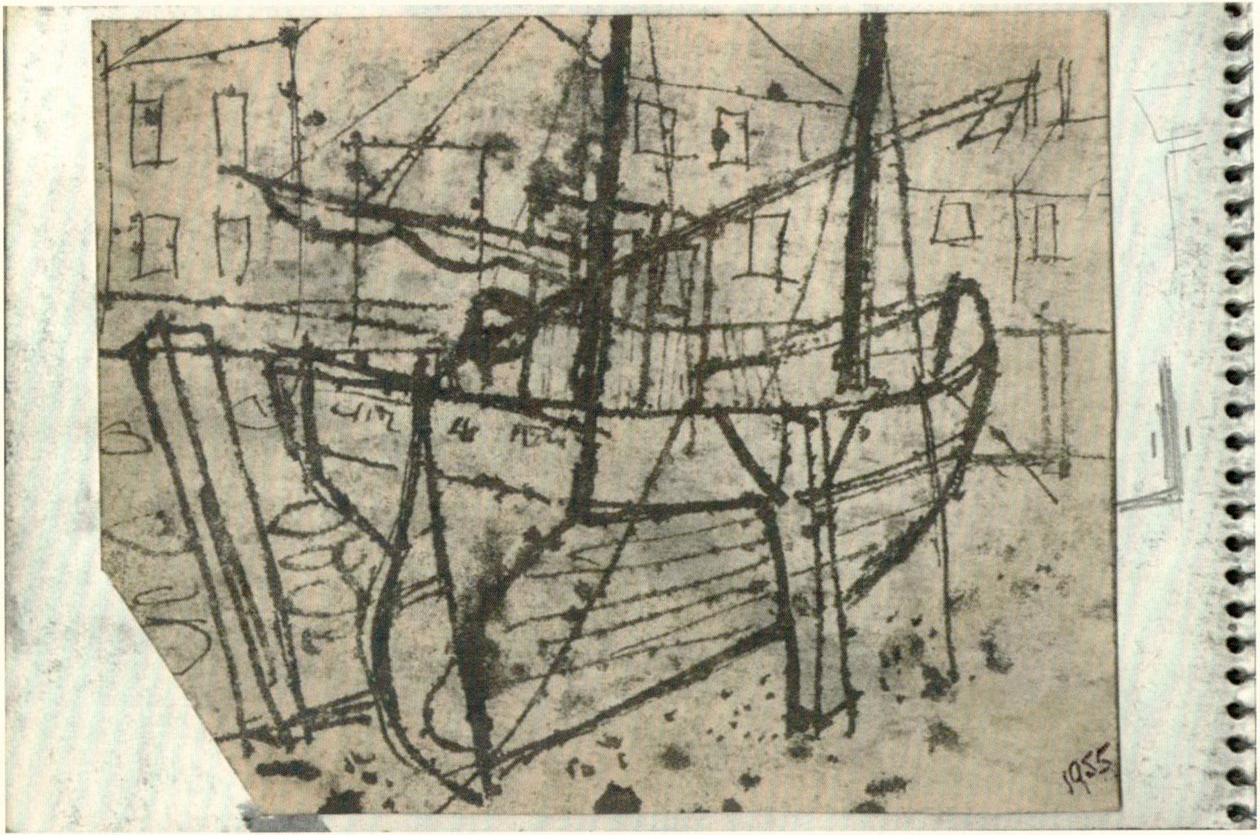
1955

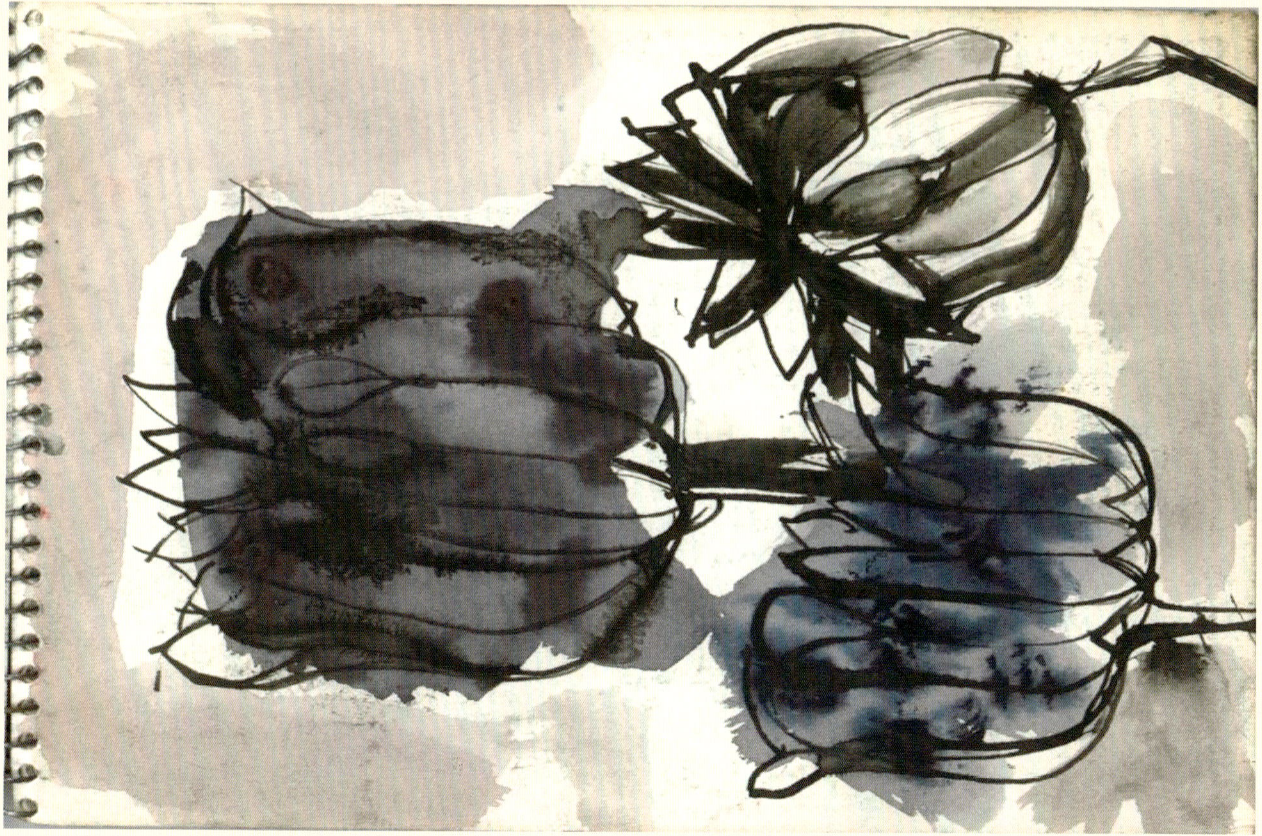

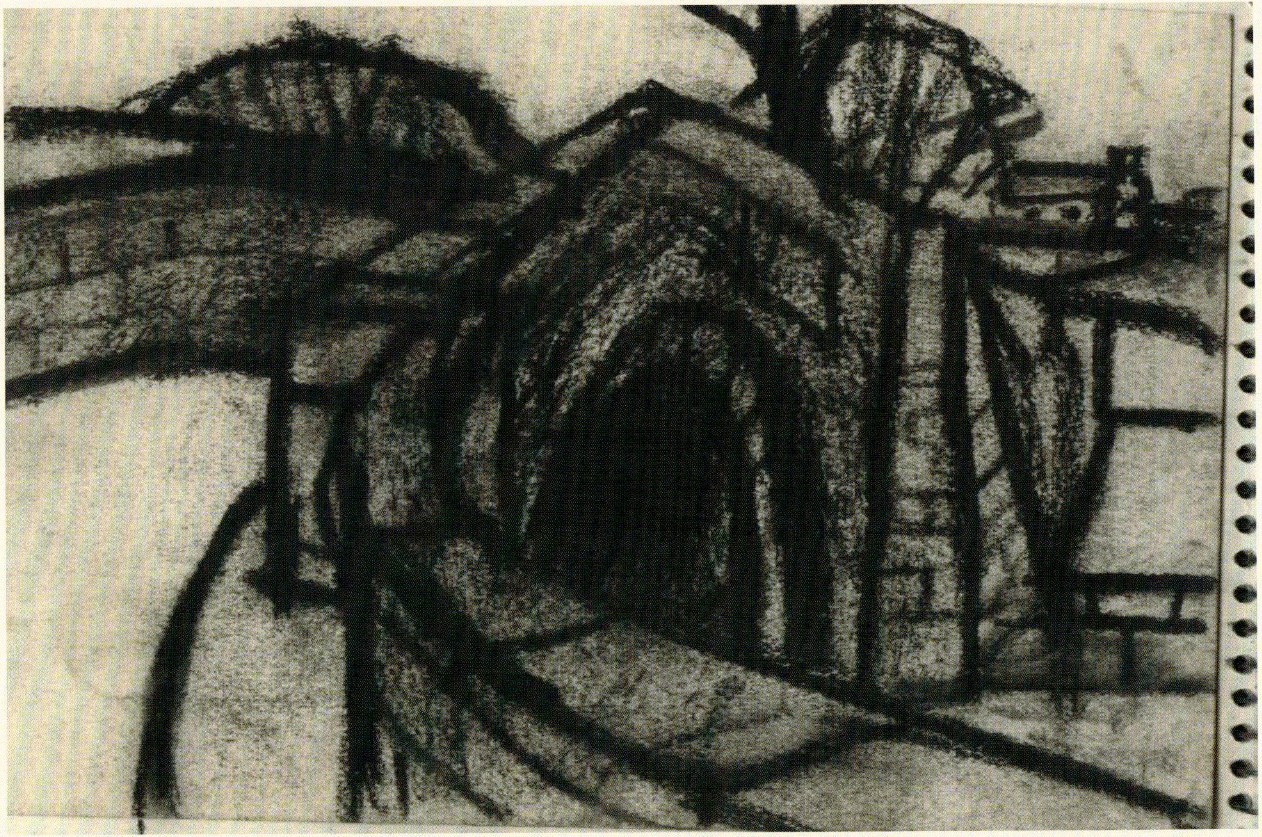

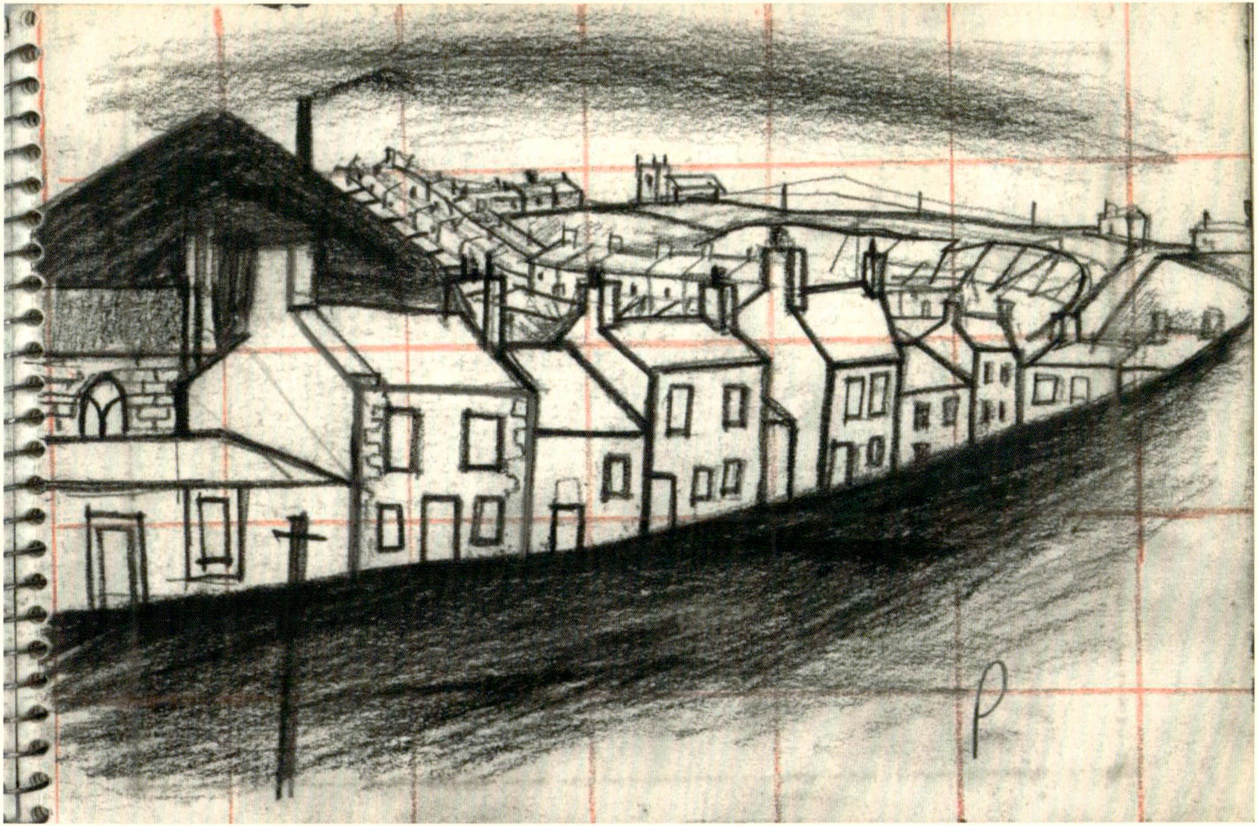

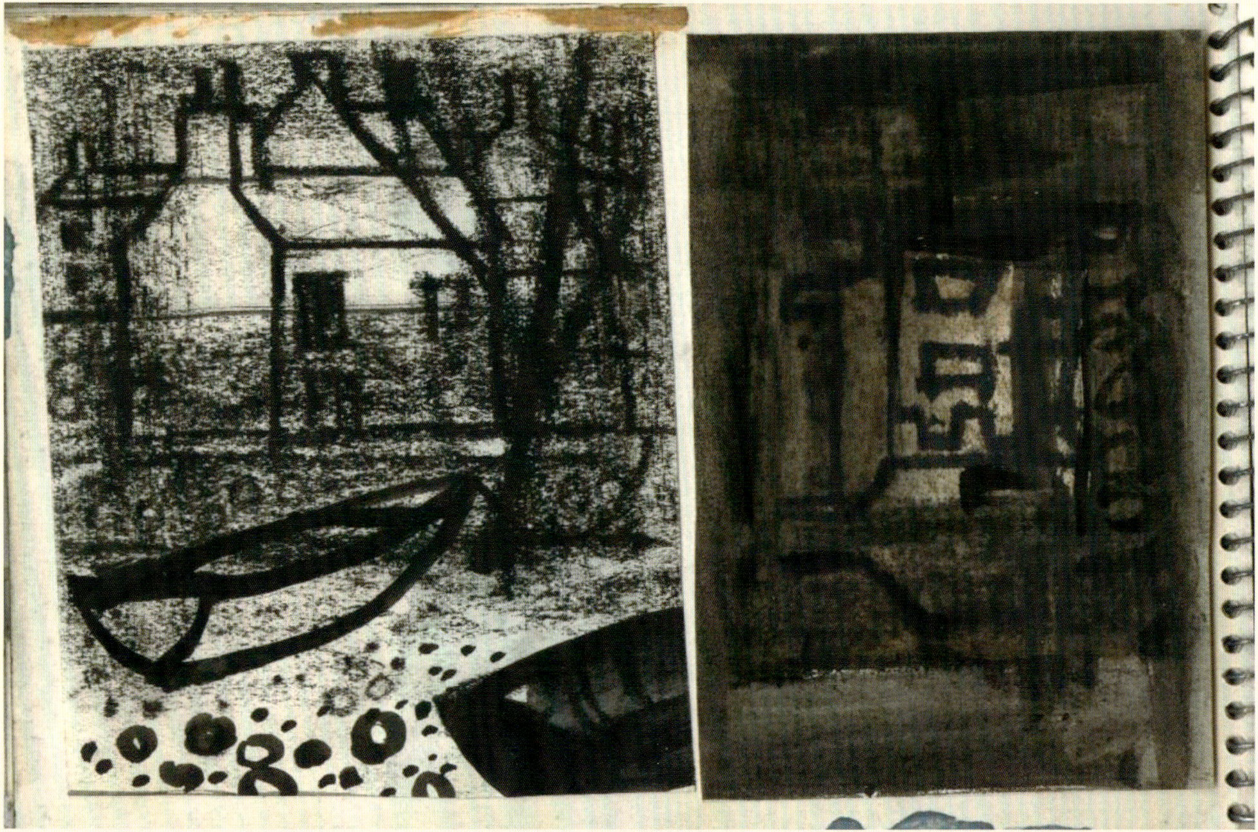

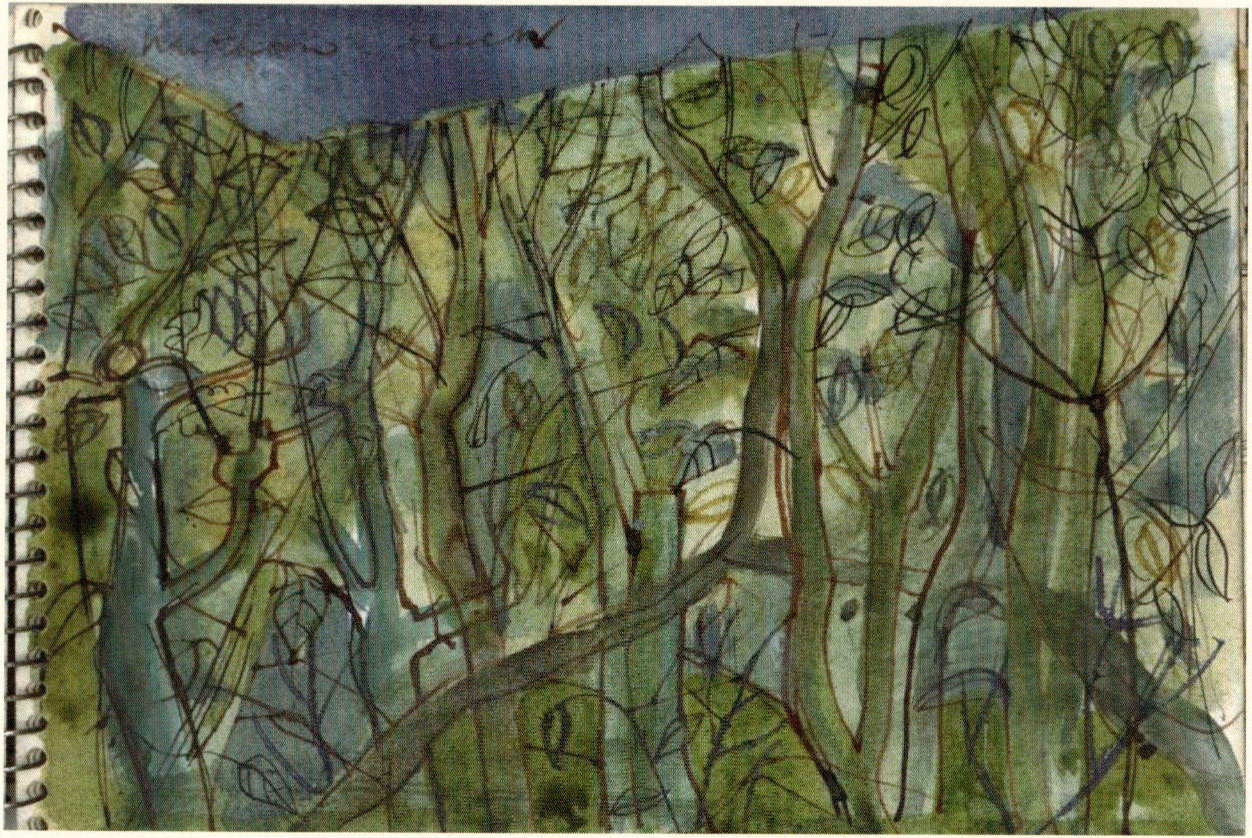

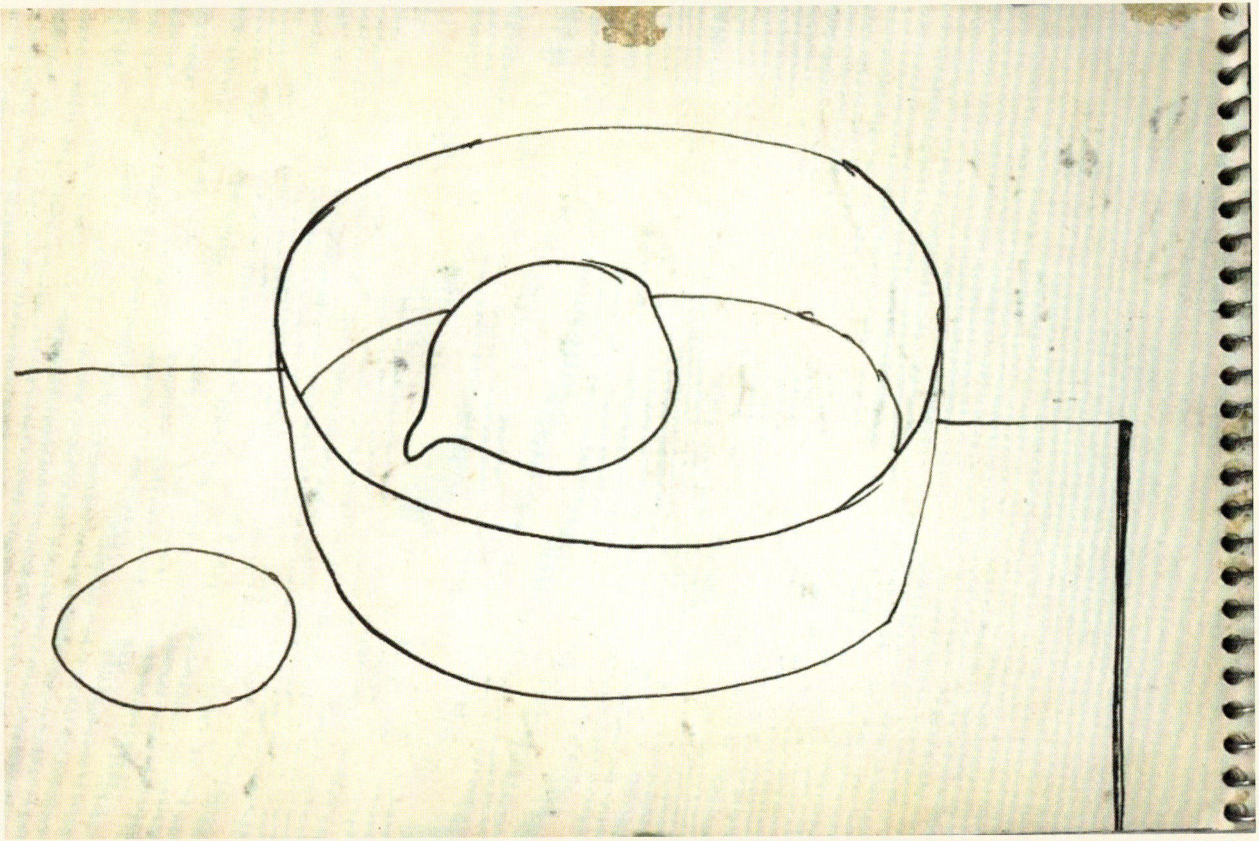

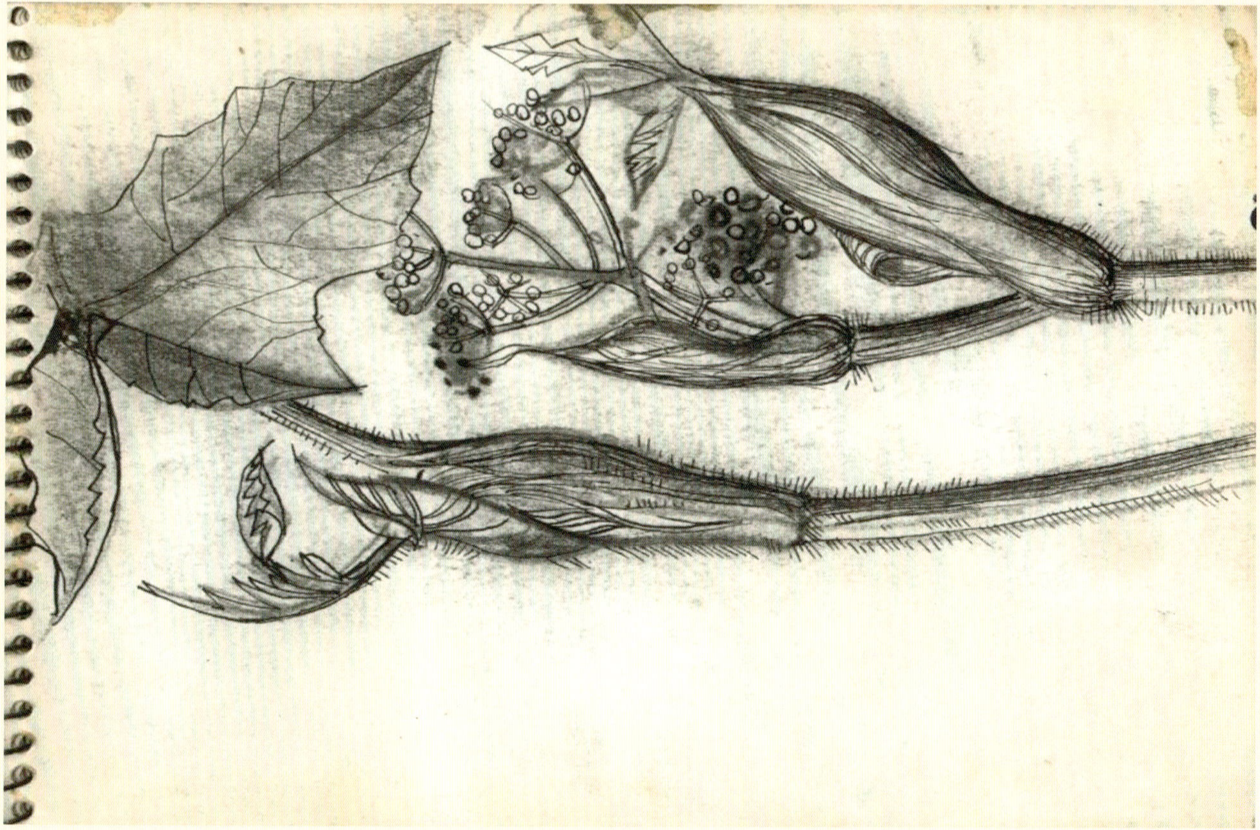

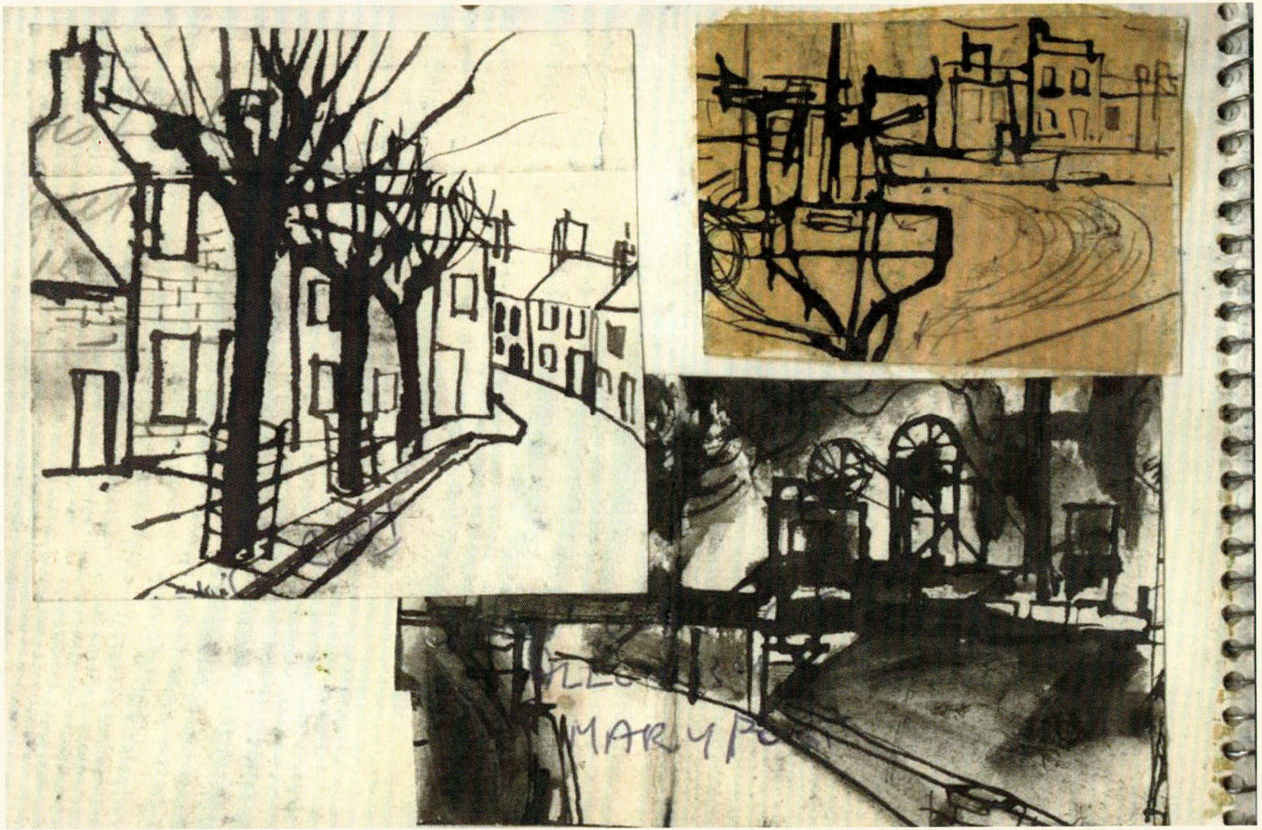

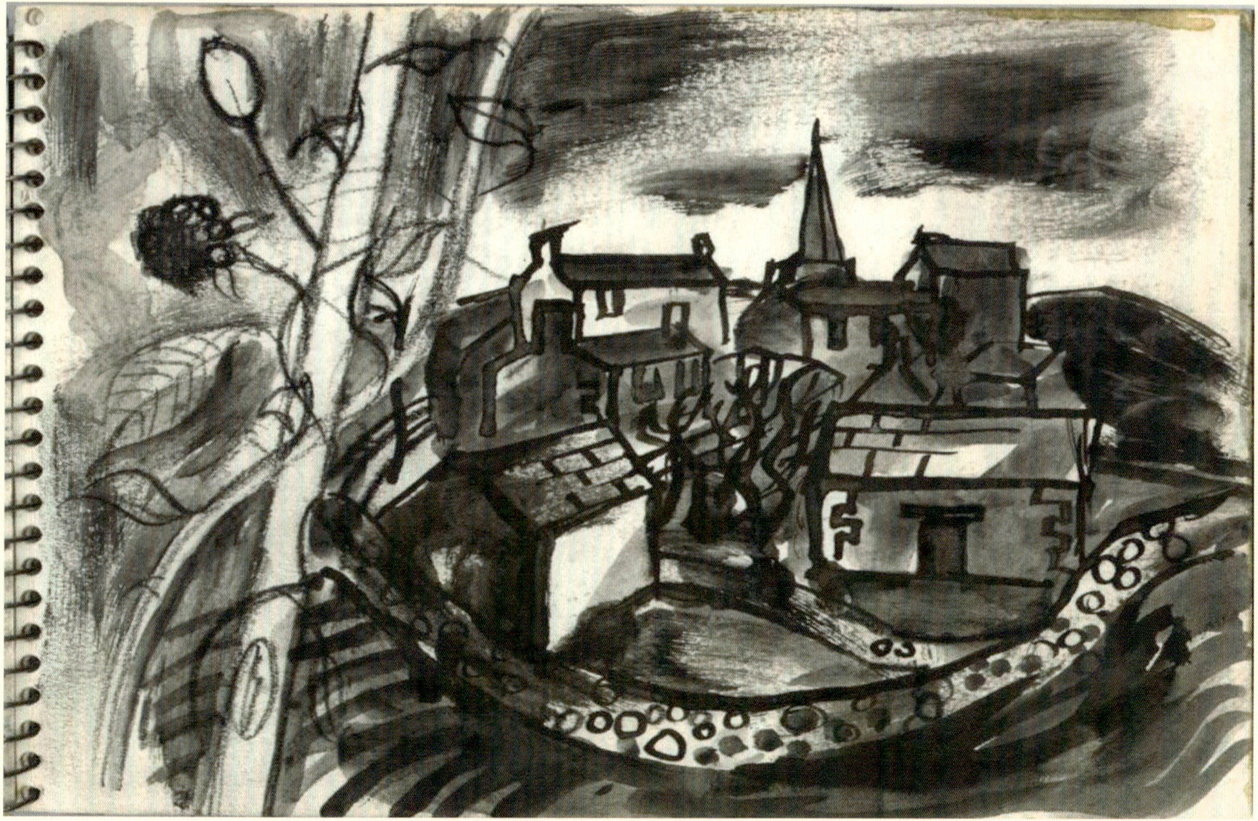

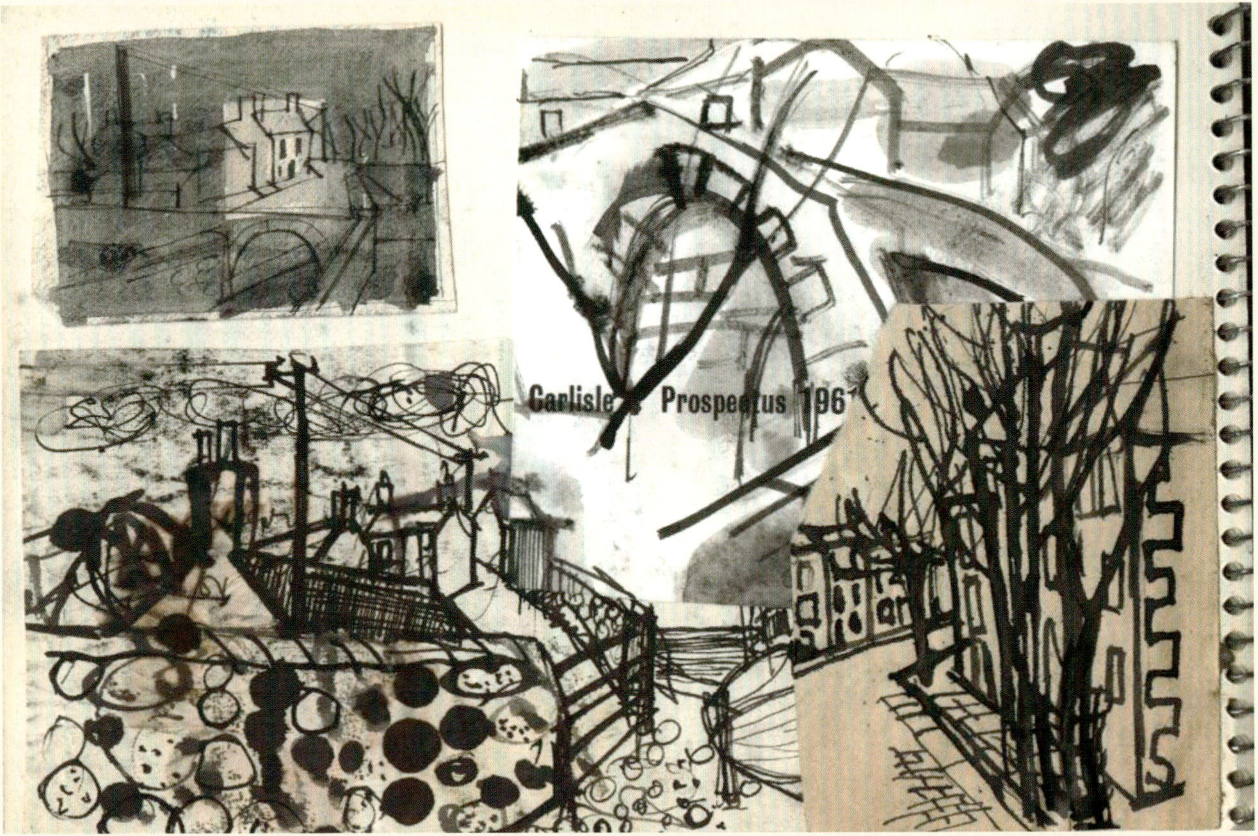
Carlisle
Prospectus 196

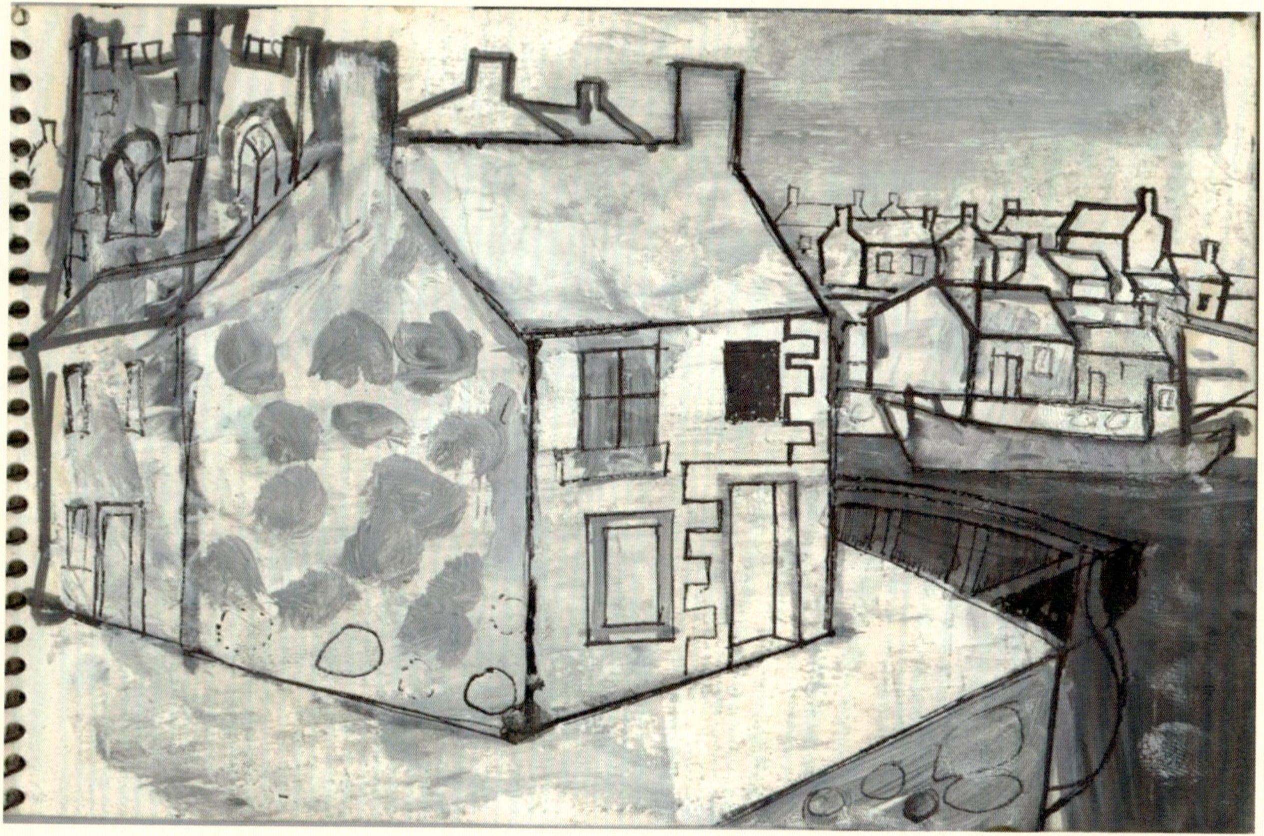

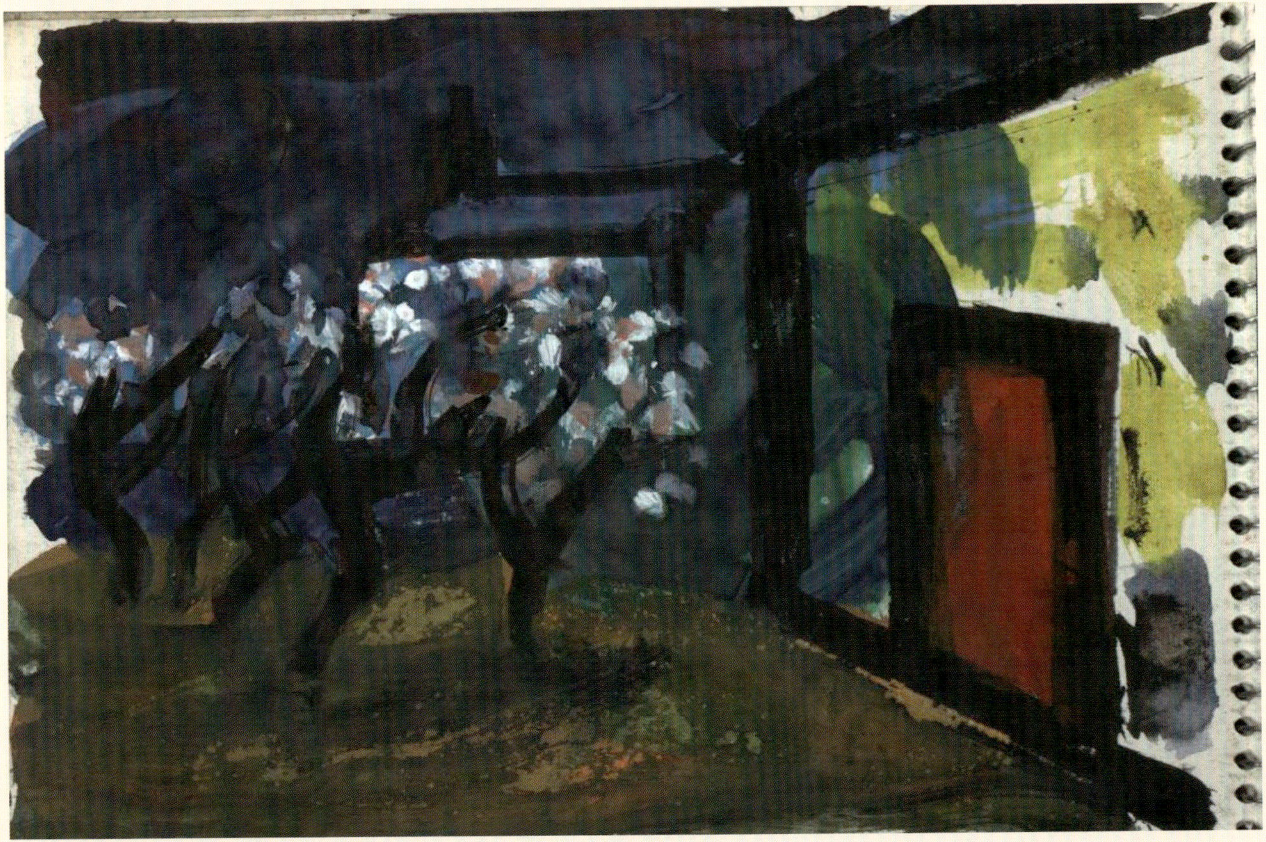

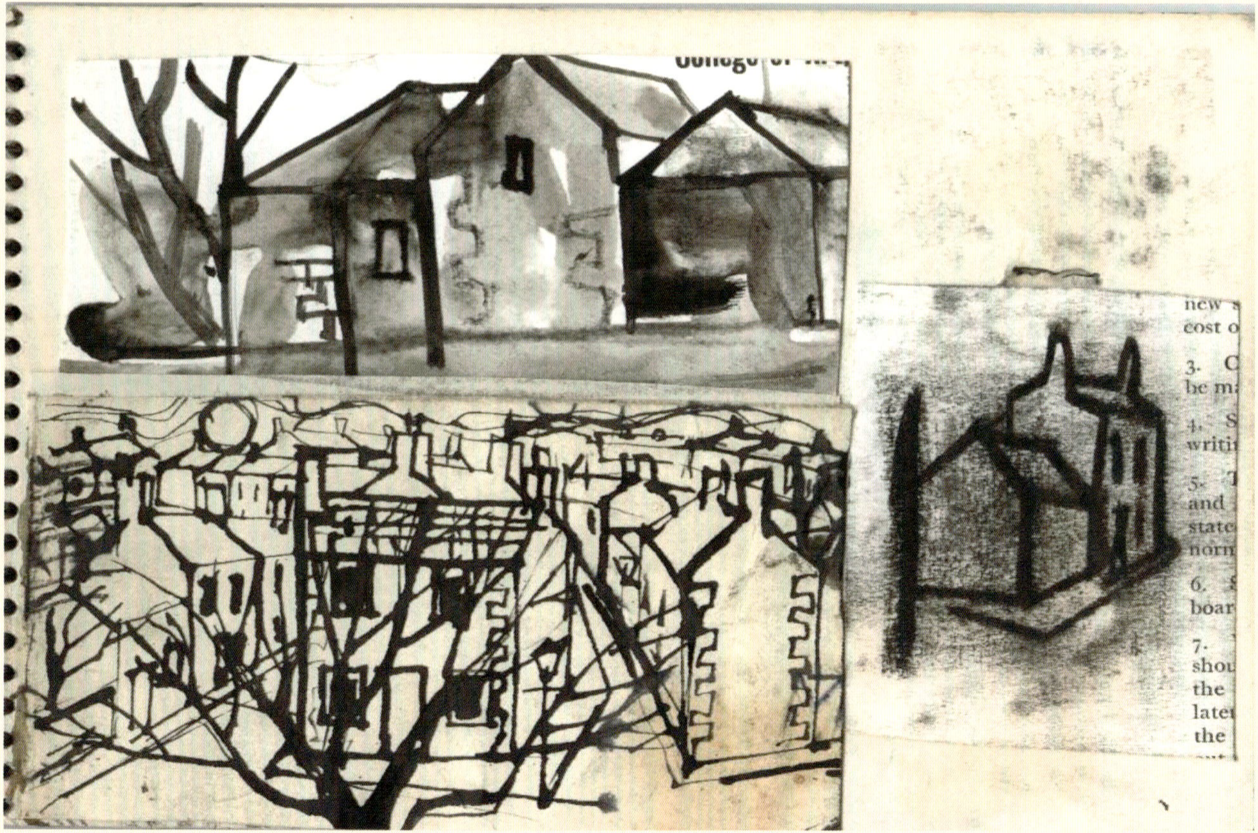

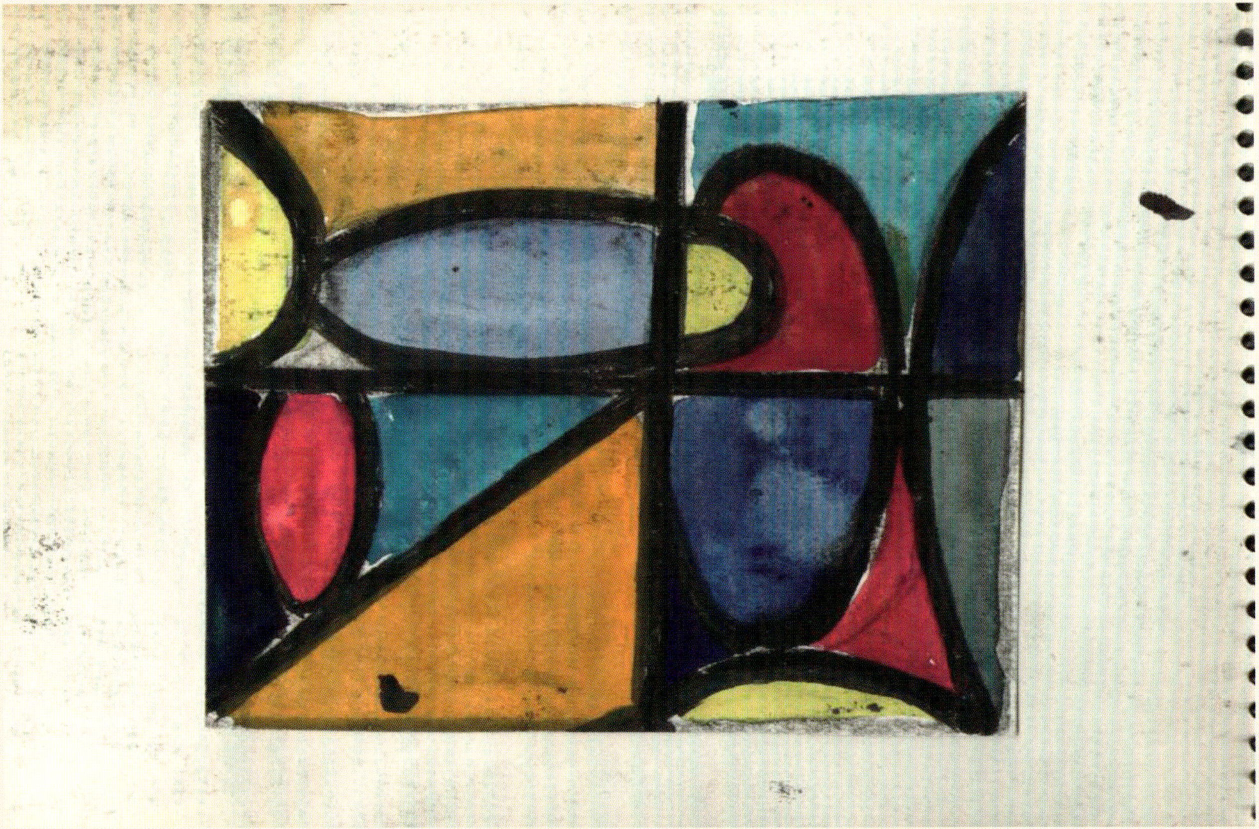

WEST CUMBERLAND VILLAGES AND COAST

Whitewash and brown paint - lovely

Rottington

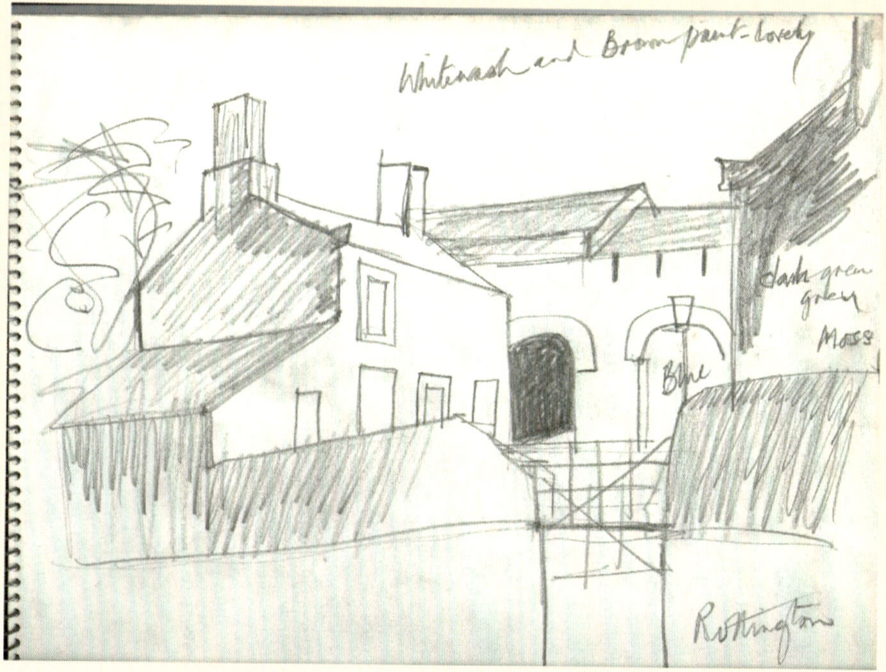

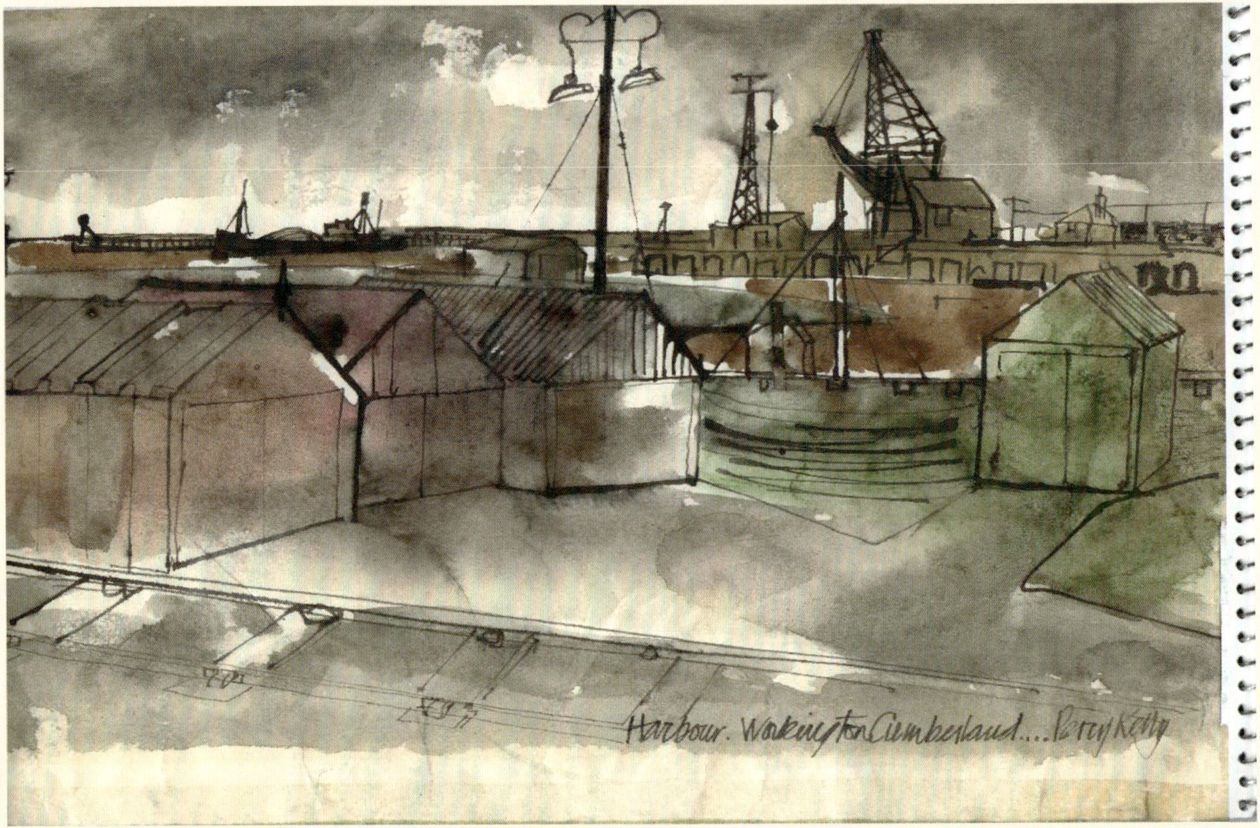

An early watercolour sketch of Workington Harbour. Kelly was born and brought up close by

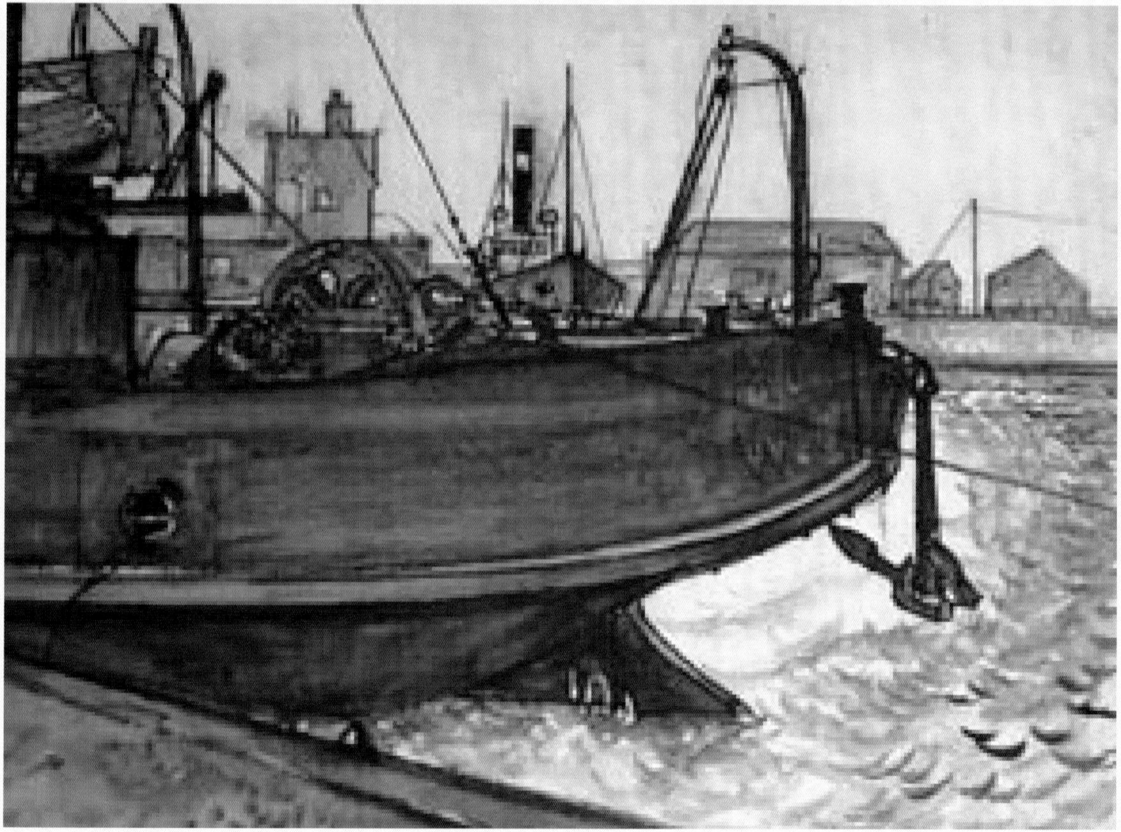

He spent many hours as a child wandering around the docks. Boats always held a fascination

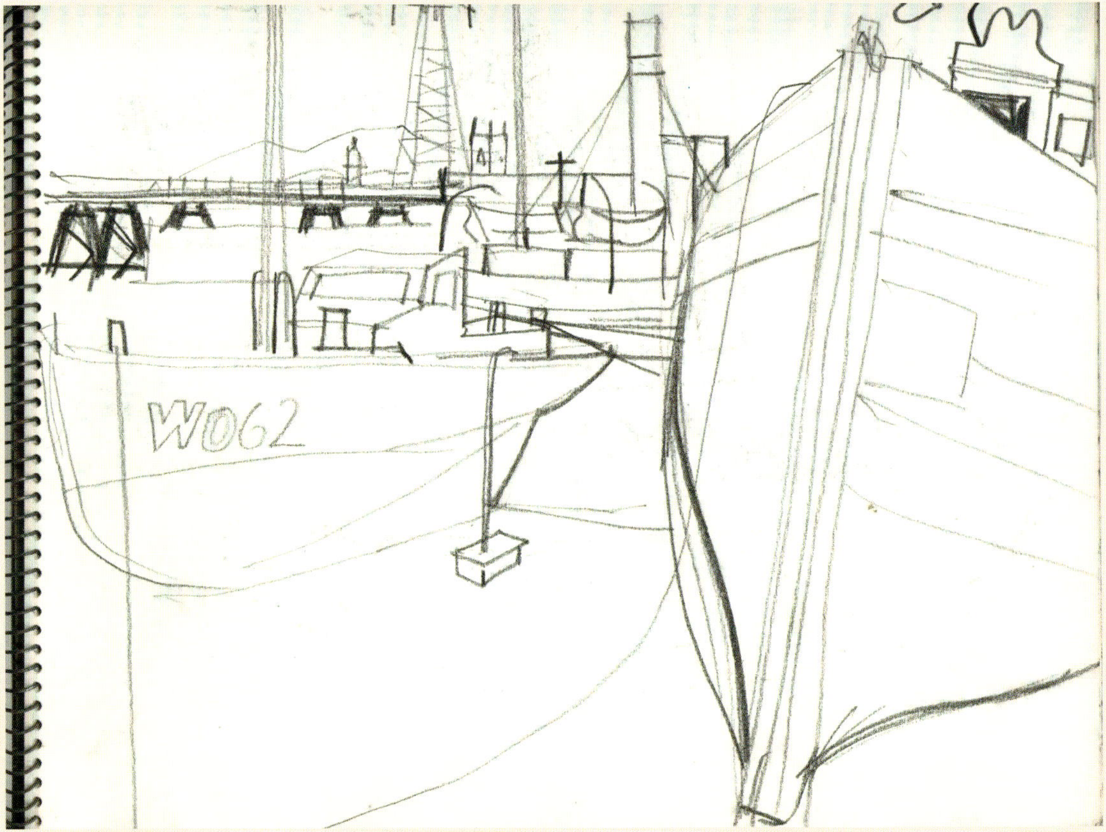

From a 1962 sketchbook

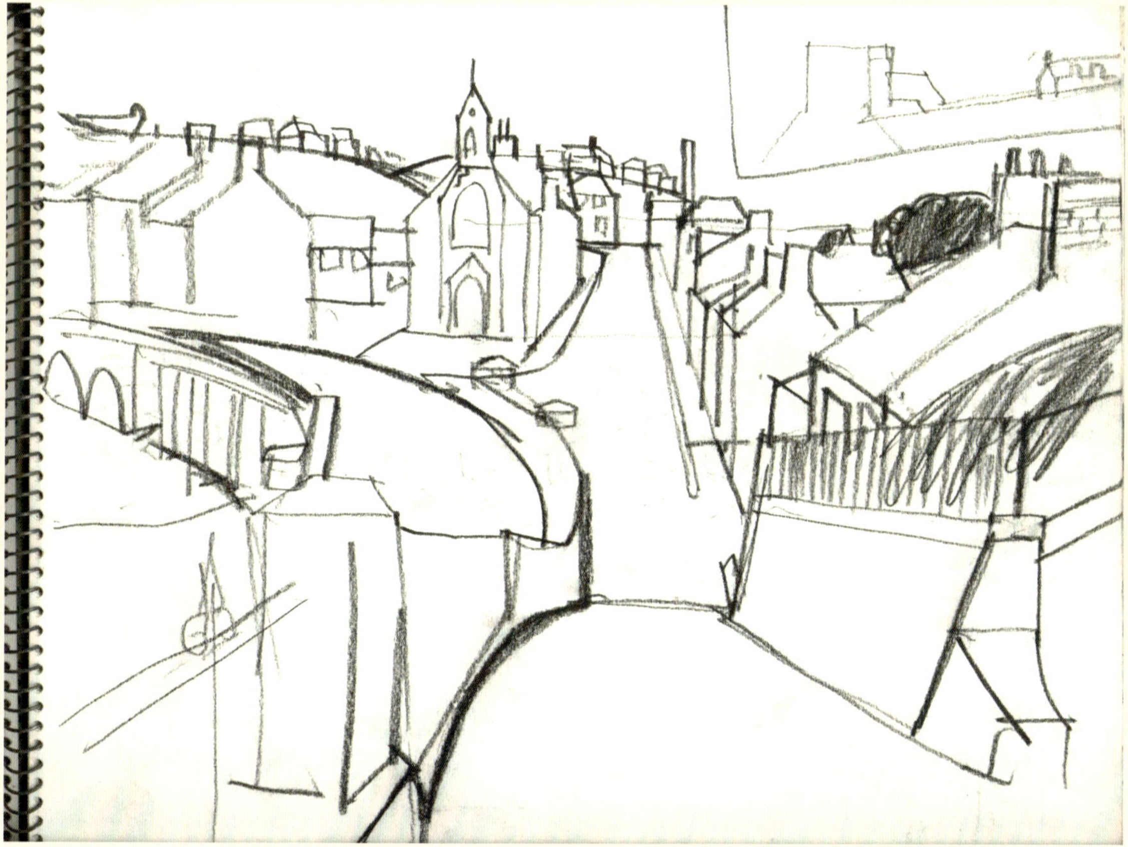
Harrington sketch from 1962 sketchbook

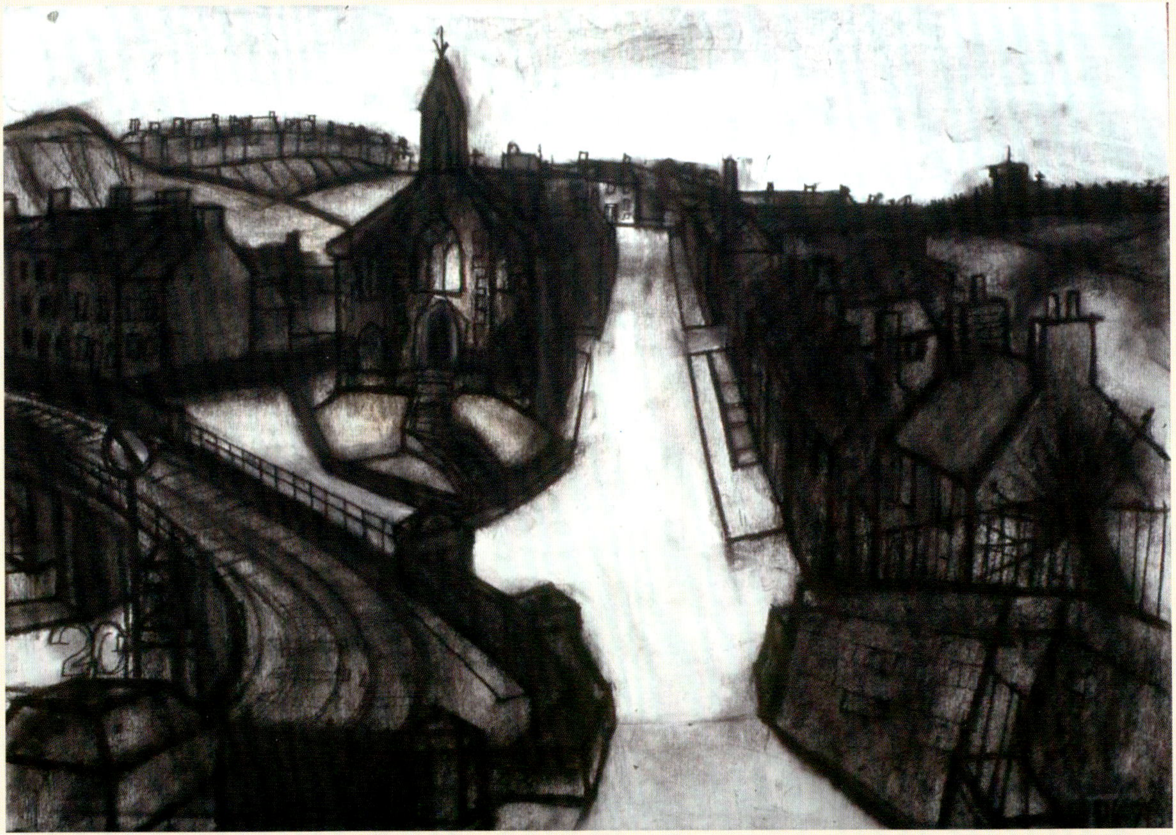

Large A2 charcoal drawing of Harrington

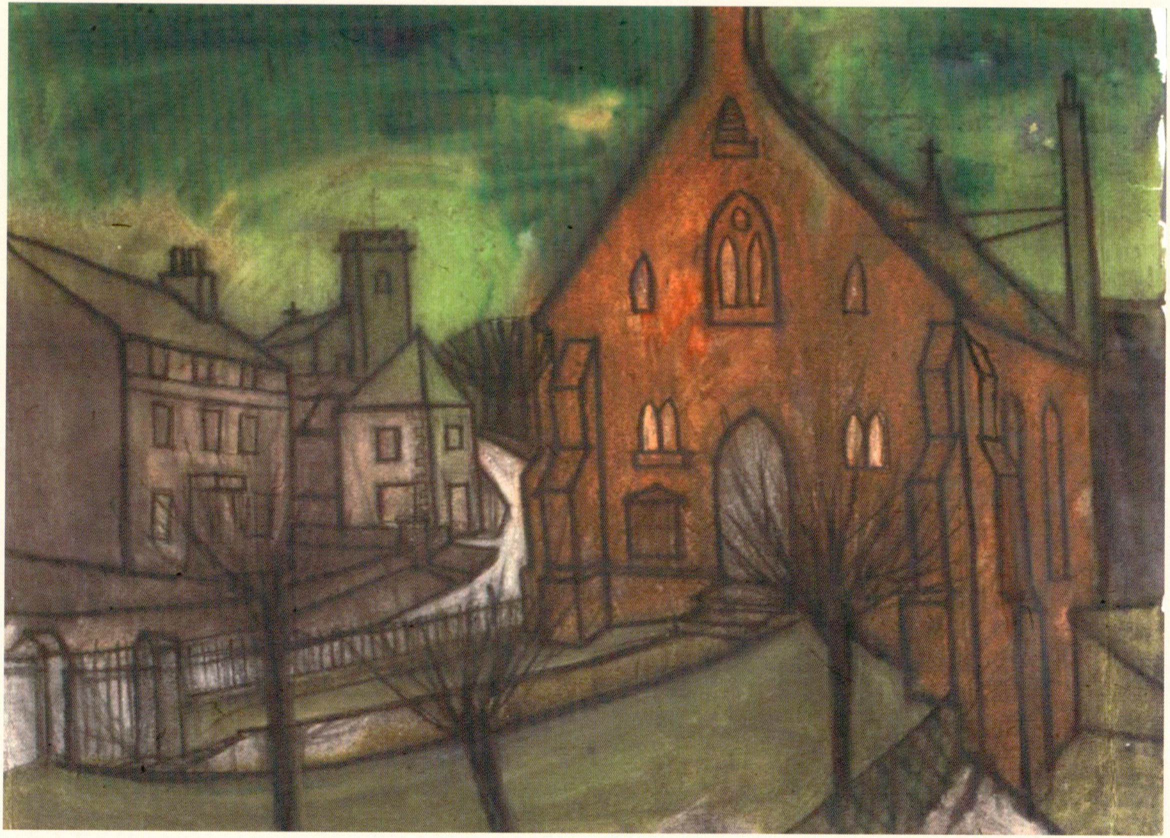

A2 painting of Harrington

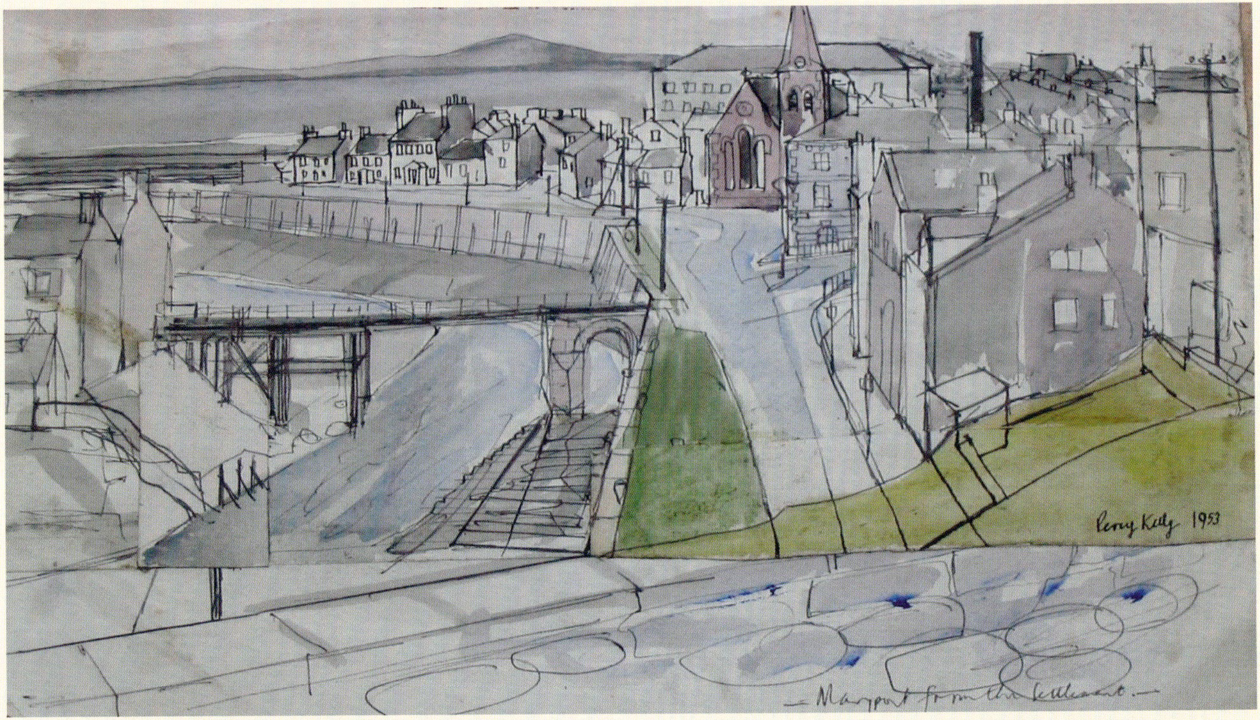

Maryport from The Settlement watercolour/pencil sketch 1953
The large painting opposite was probably made many years later from ear;ier sketches

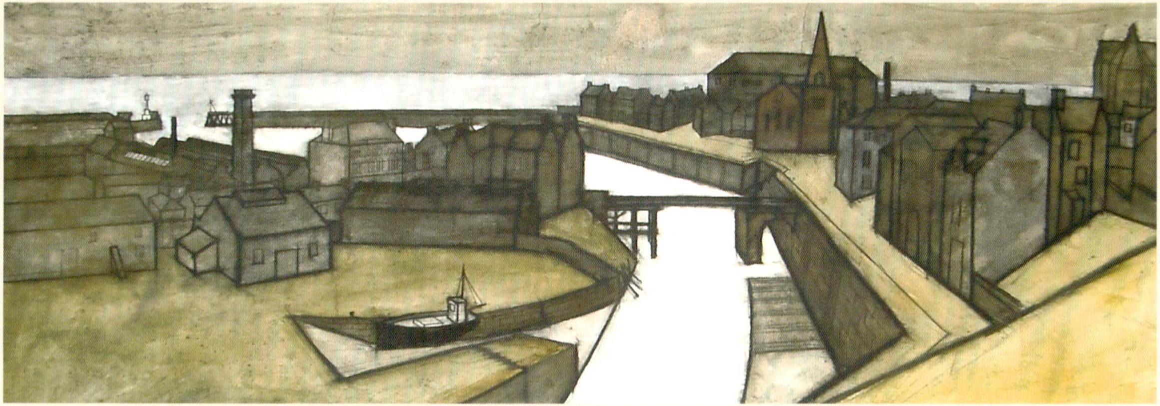

Maryport from the Settlement Watercolour 72″ x 30″

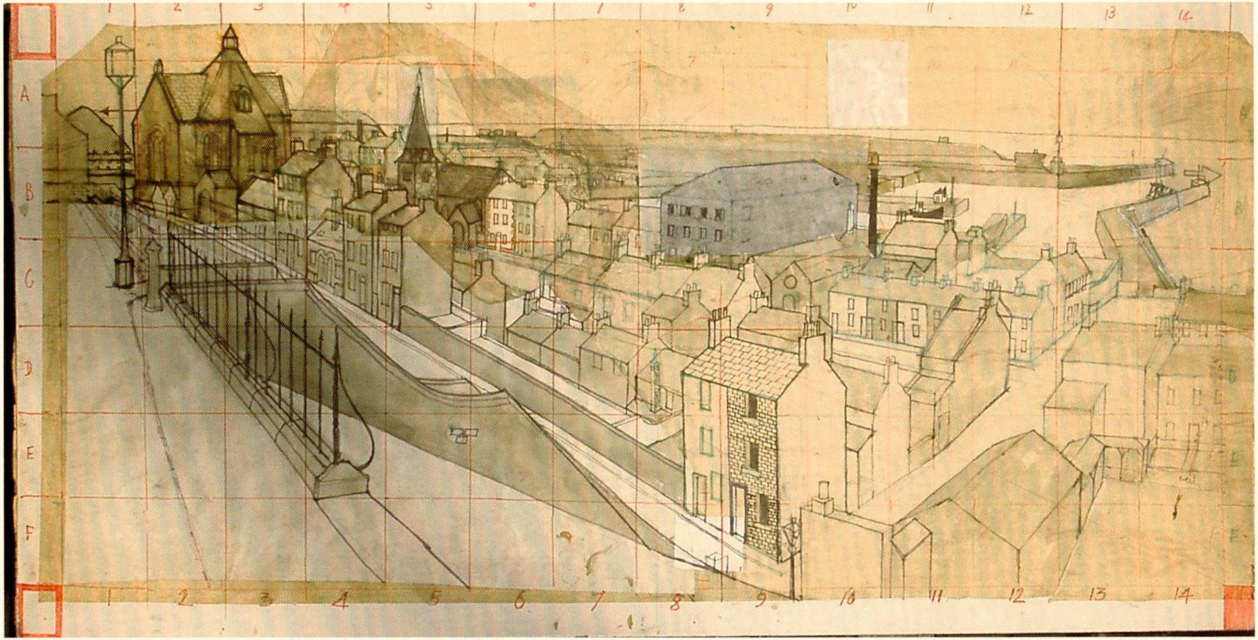

This is the rough sketch for Maryport from the North made on the back of a 30″ x 15″piece of card used for cutting. Corrections have been made by sticking pieces on.

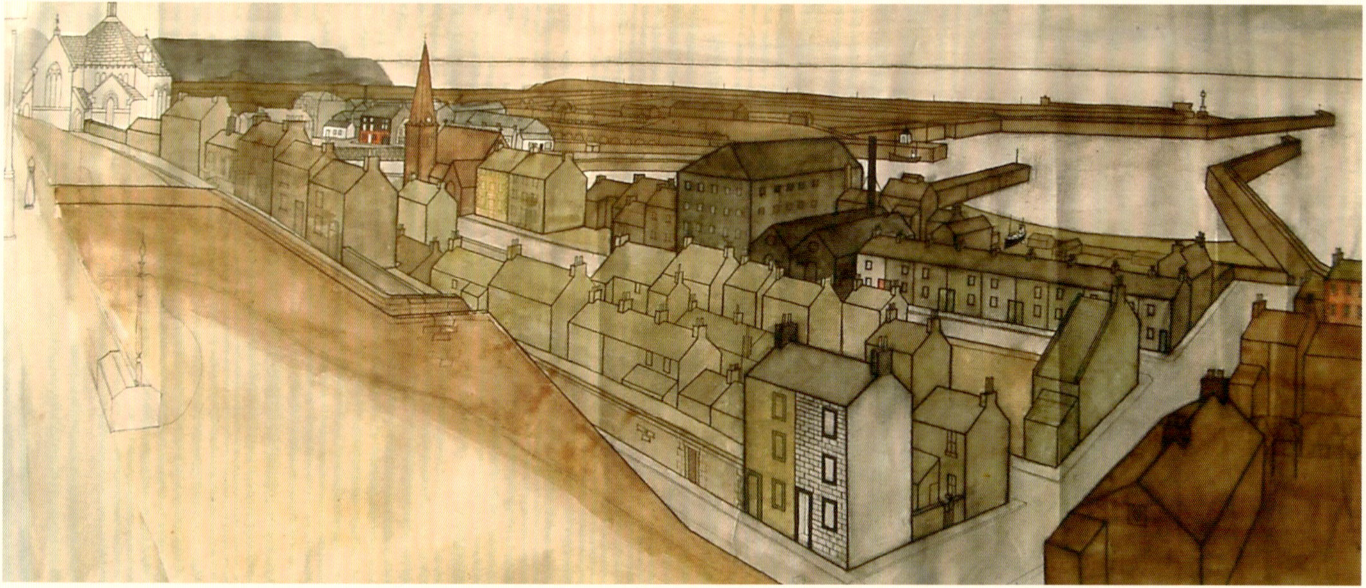

Maryport from the North Watercolour/ink 72″ x 30″

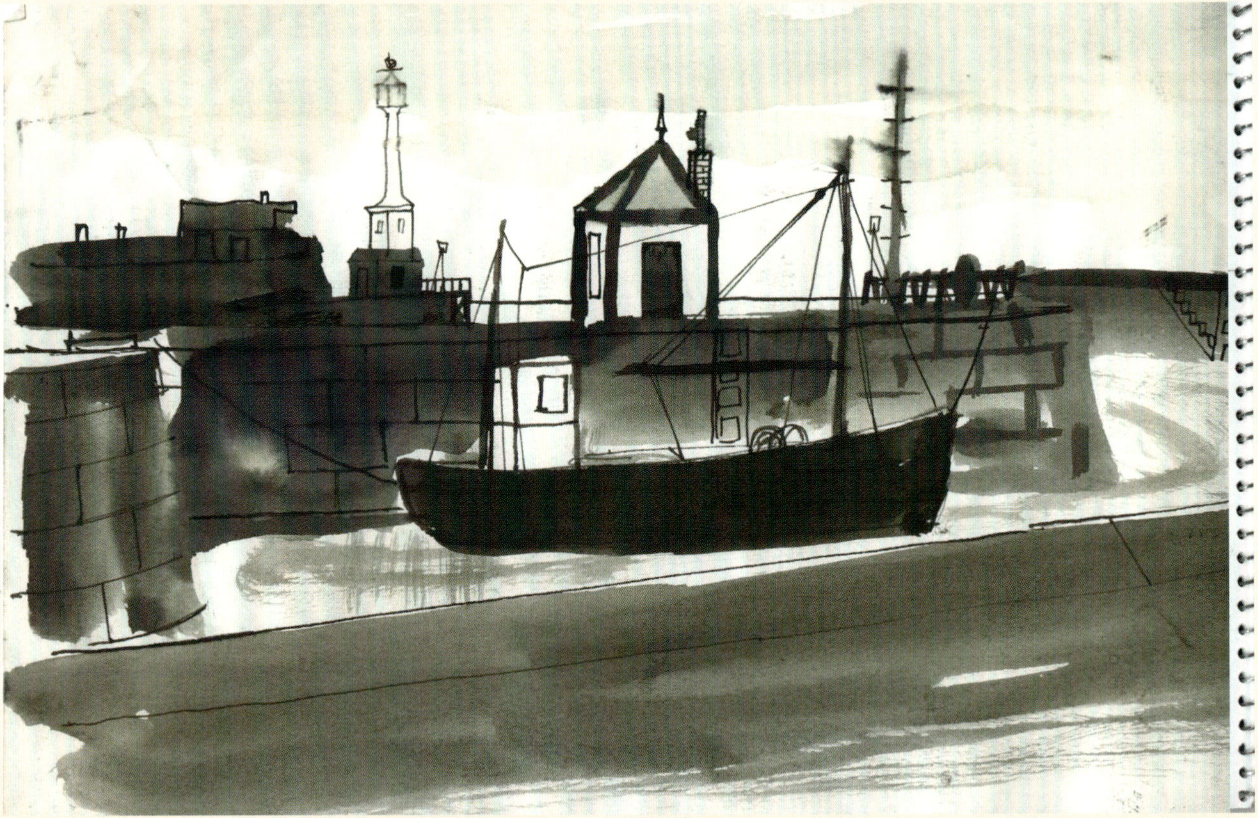

Sketch for Red Boat

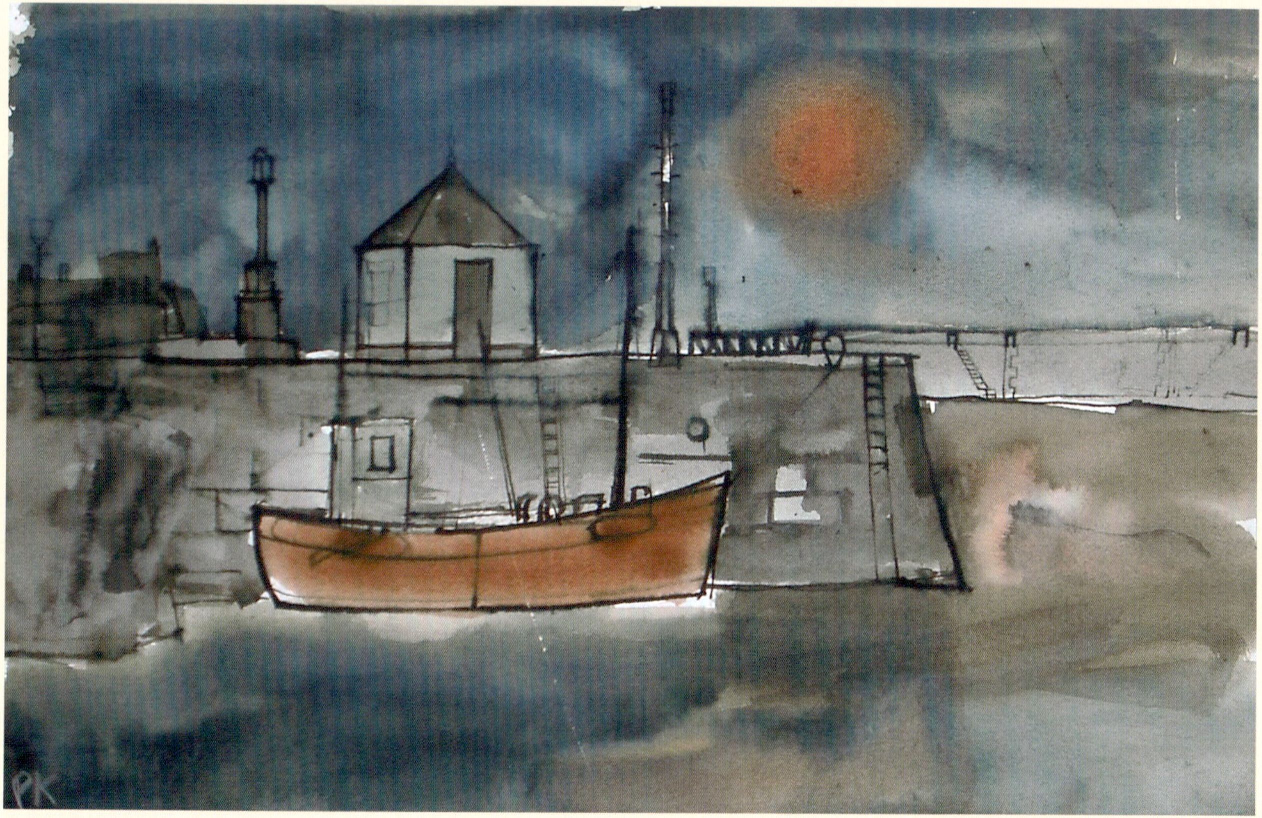

Red boat Watercolour painting

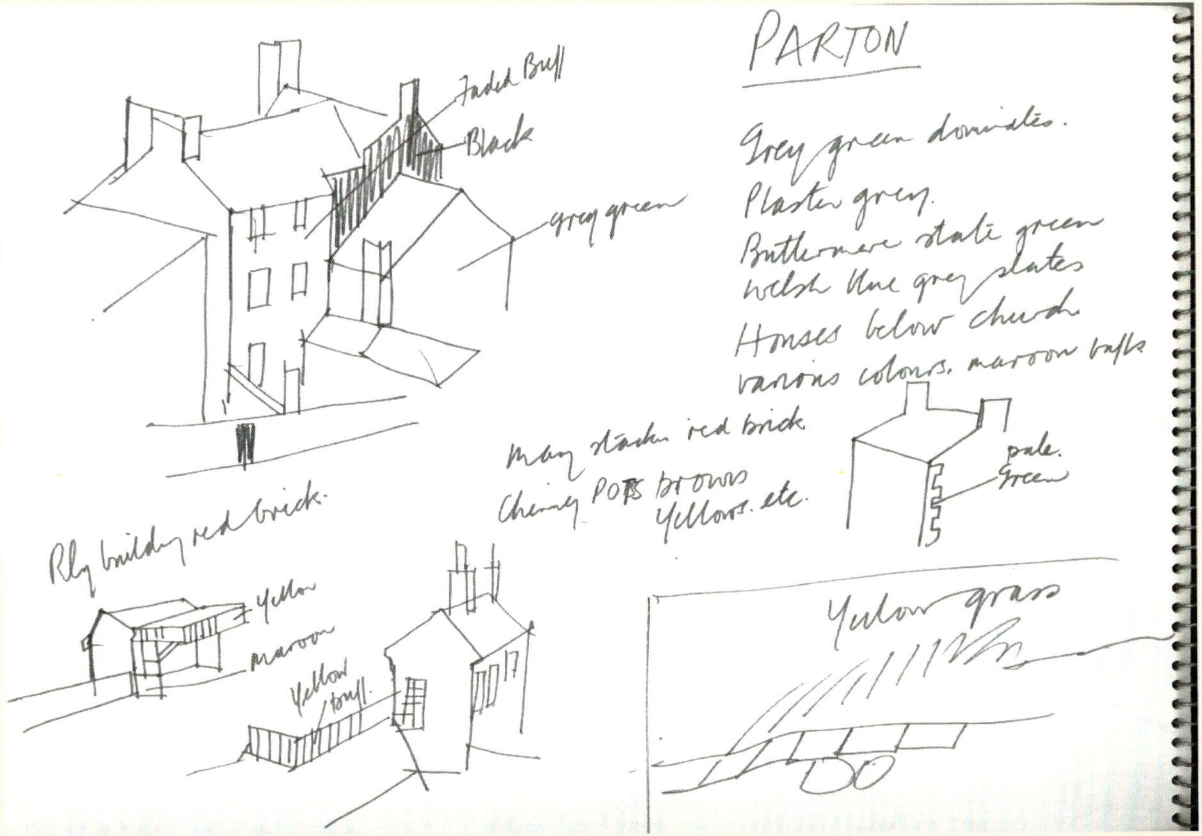

After Kelly left college in 1965, he became a protégé of Sir Nicholas Sekers and his family at Rosehill near Whitehaven. He spent a lot of time drawing around Moresby, Parton and Lowca as well as Whitehaven.

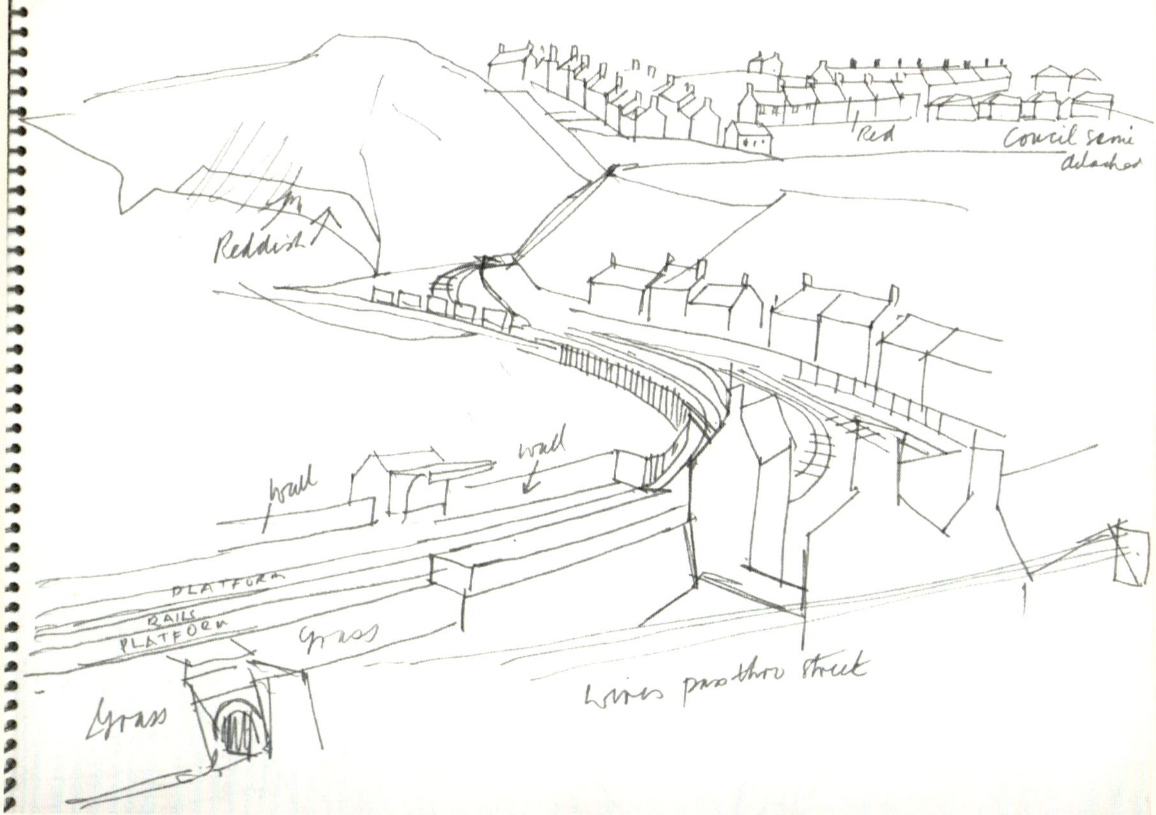

Parton became one of his favourite places for sketching.

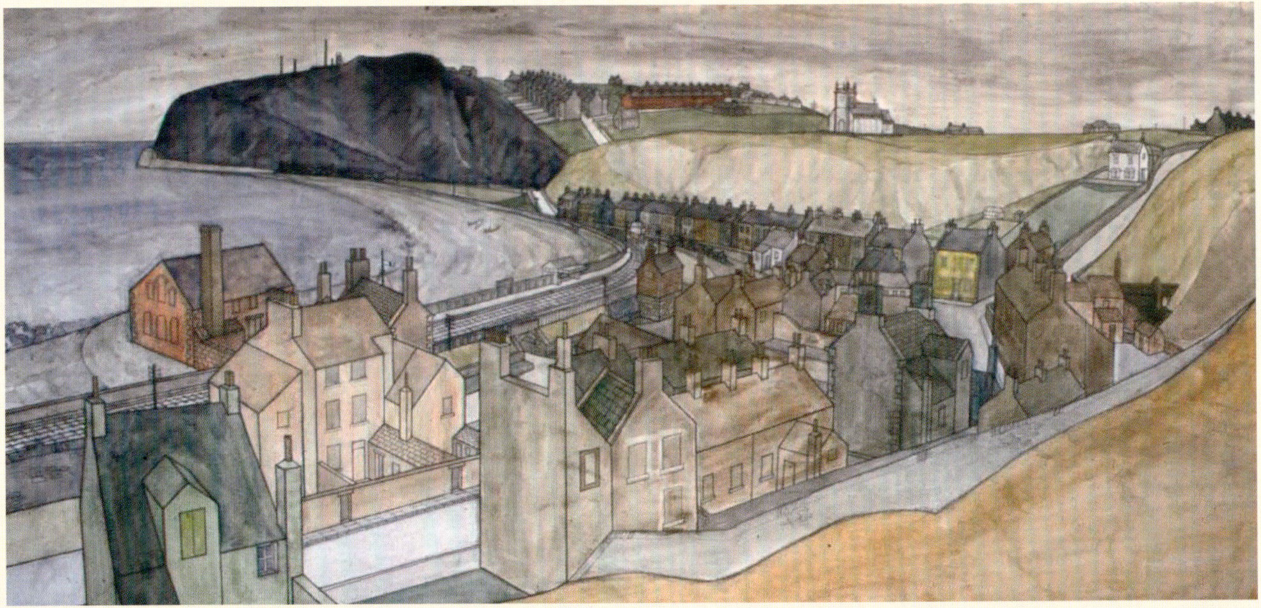

This large (76" x 36") painting of Parton and Lowca is now in the Government's National Collection

LAKE DISTRICT LANDSCAPE

Though Percy Kelly preferred the industrial coastline, terraces and villages of West Cumbria, he enjoyed the landscape of the Lake District. He spent happy days wandering the fells and valleys, particularly Newlands, the Vale of Lorton and the Loweswater area.

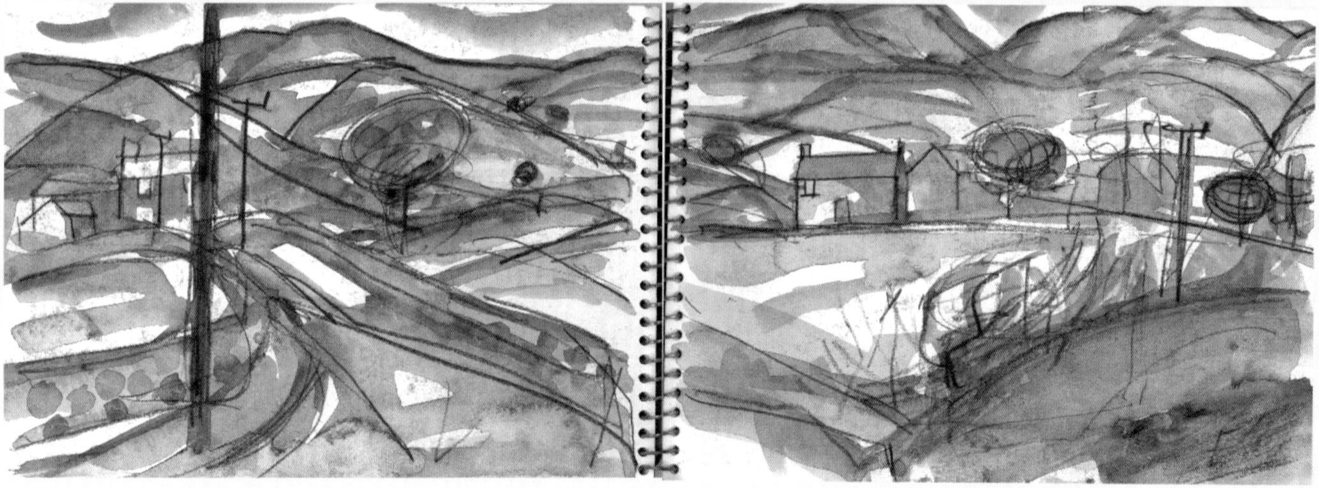

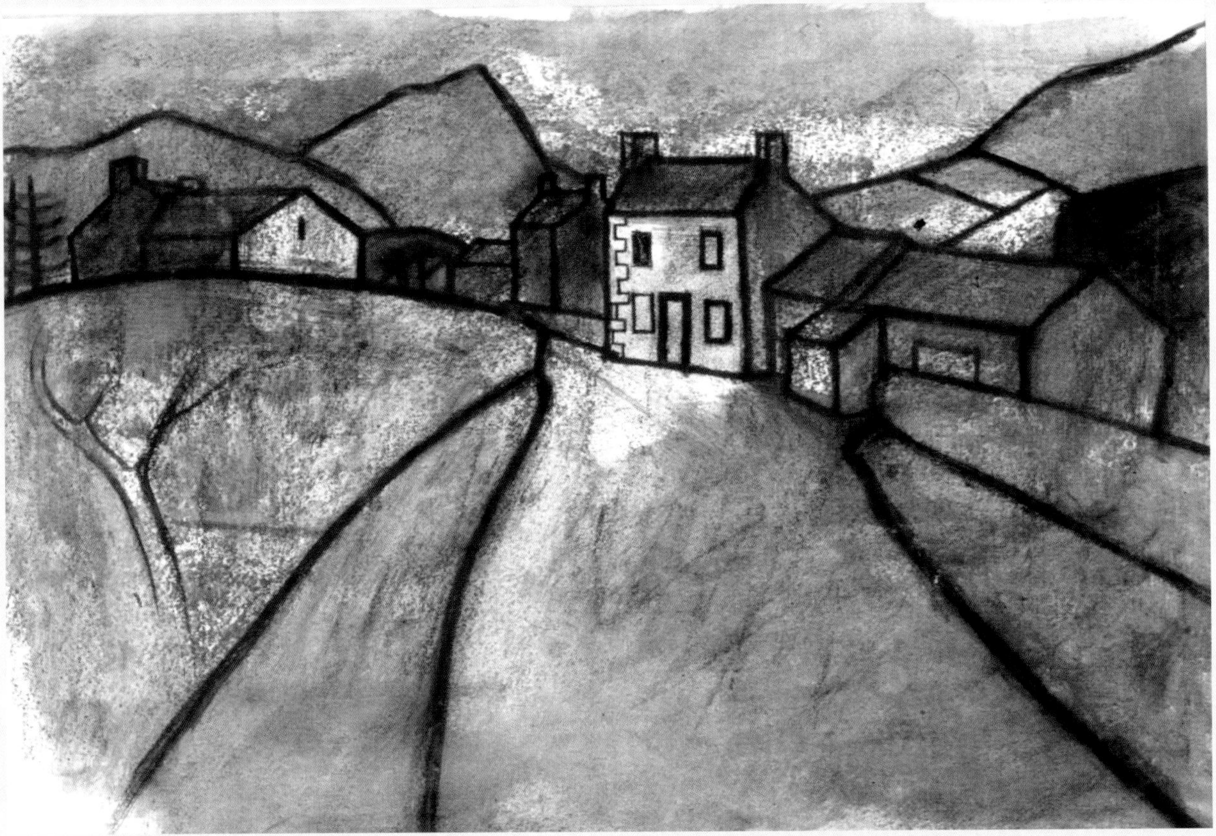

A sketch of one of his favourite corners of Low Lorton

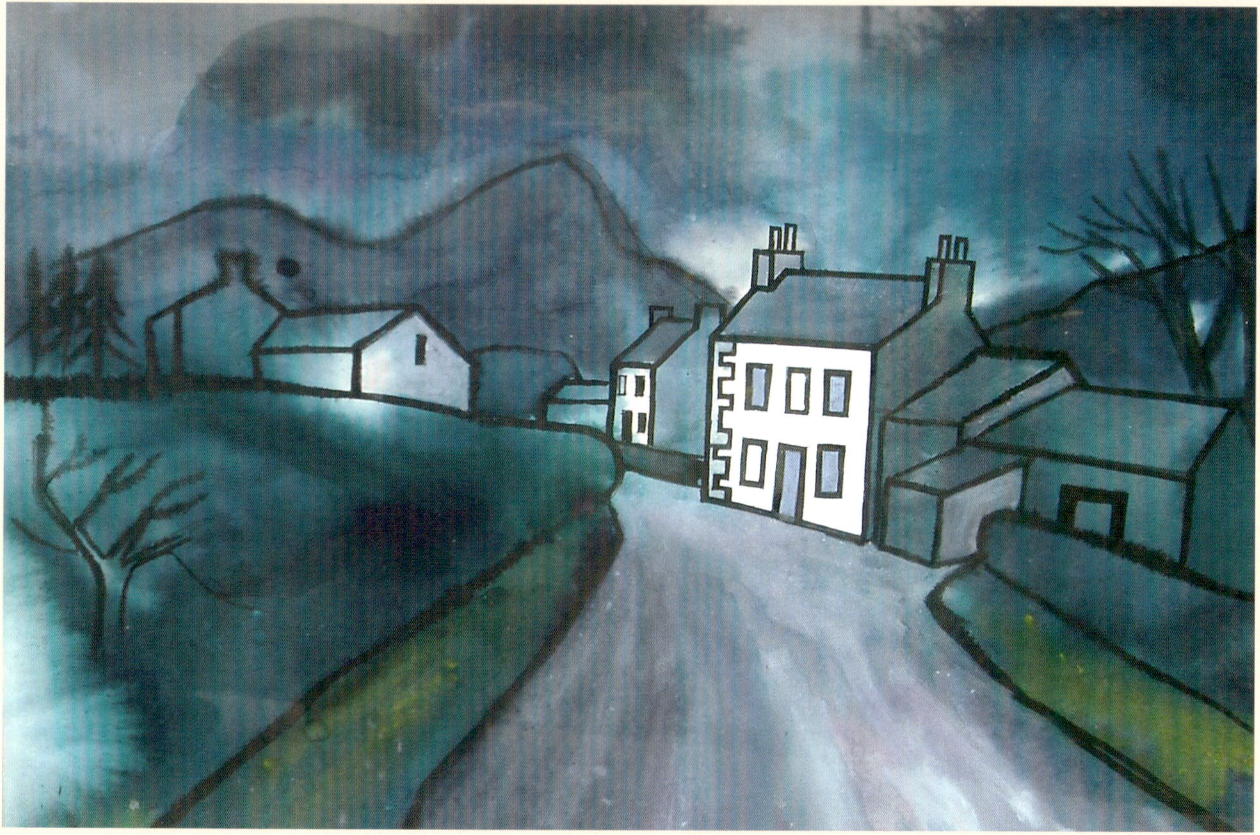

White Cottage, Lorton Watercolour/ink

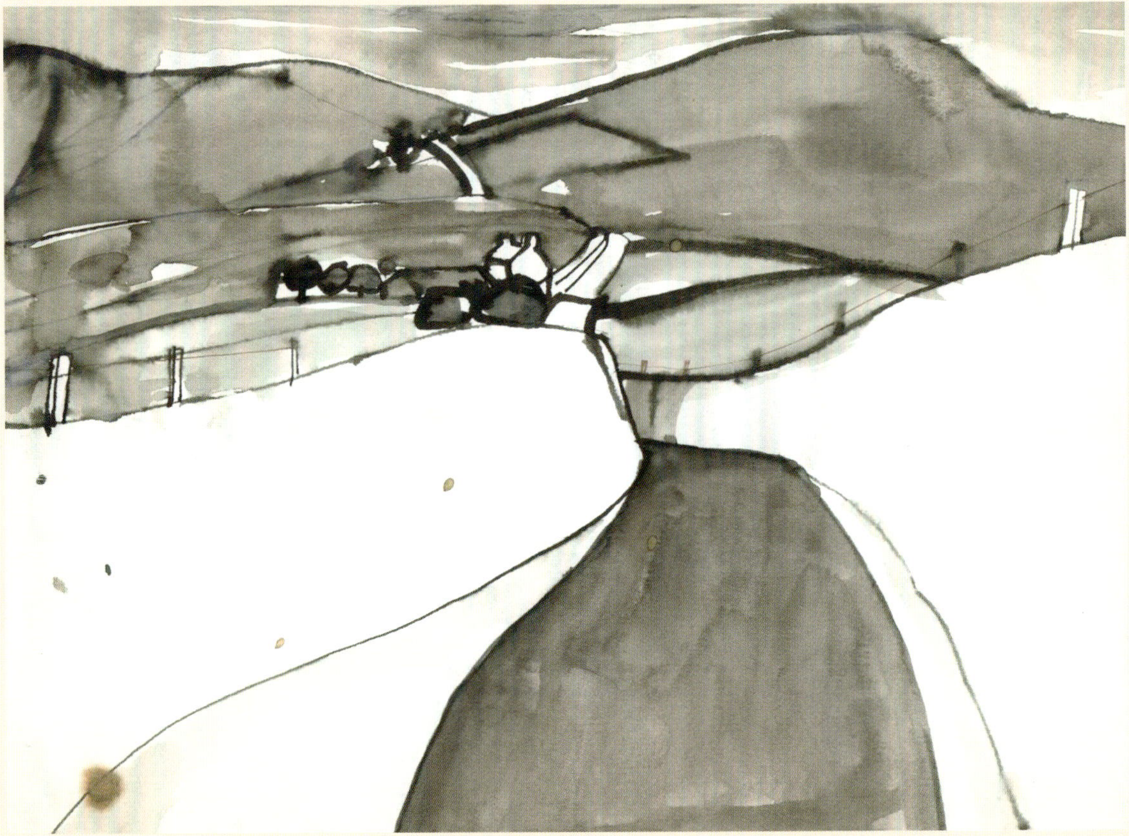

Sketch for White Cottage

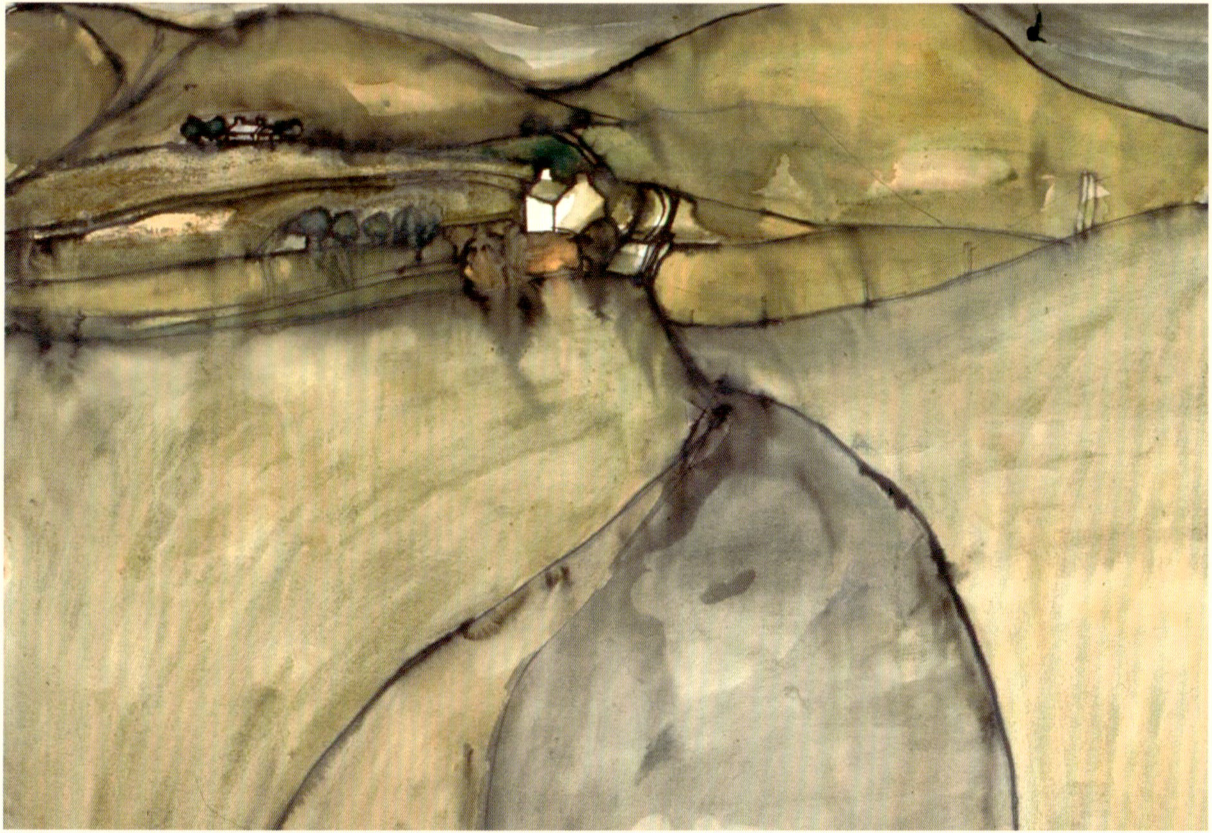

White cottage

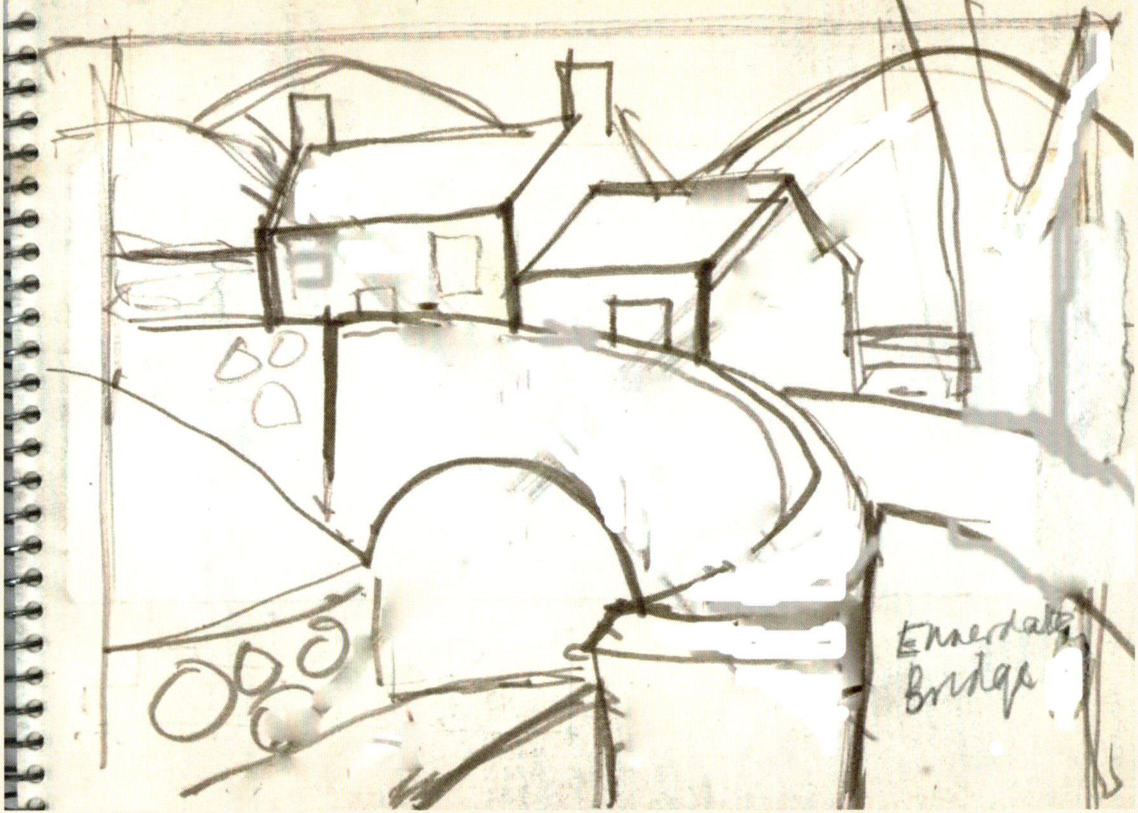

Ennerdale Bridge

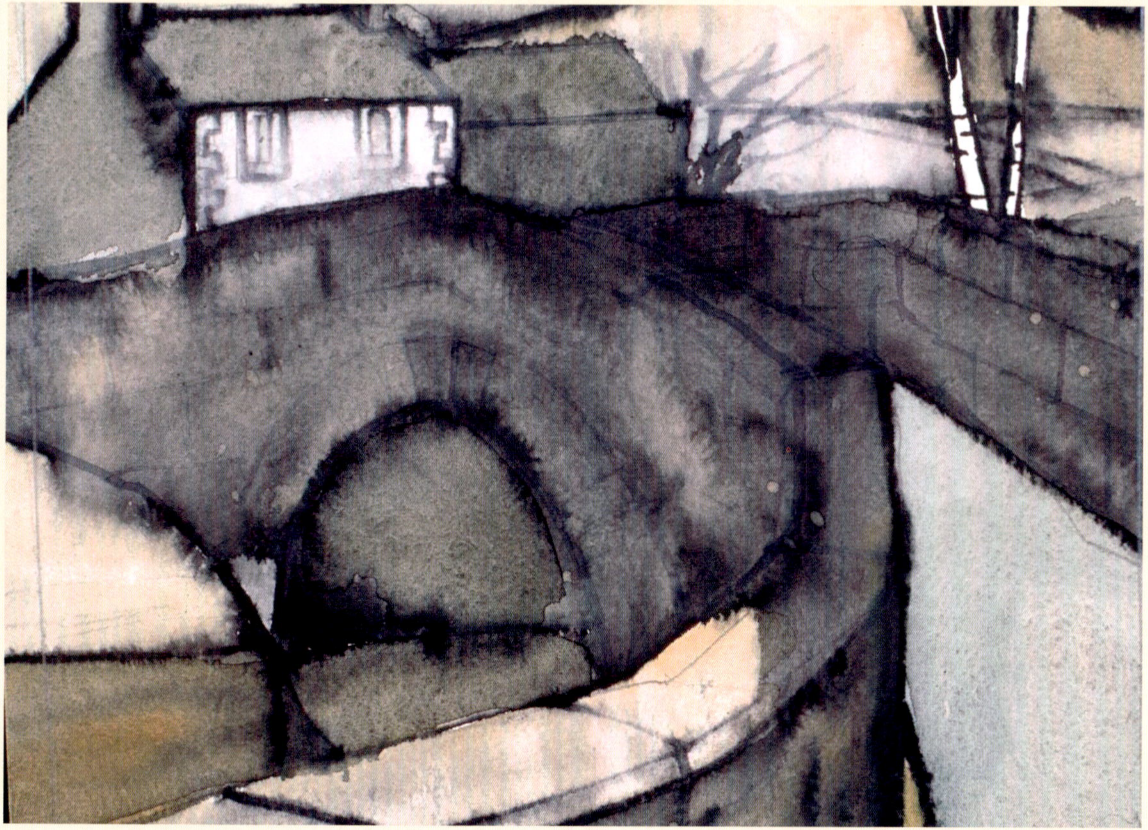

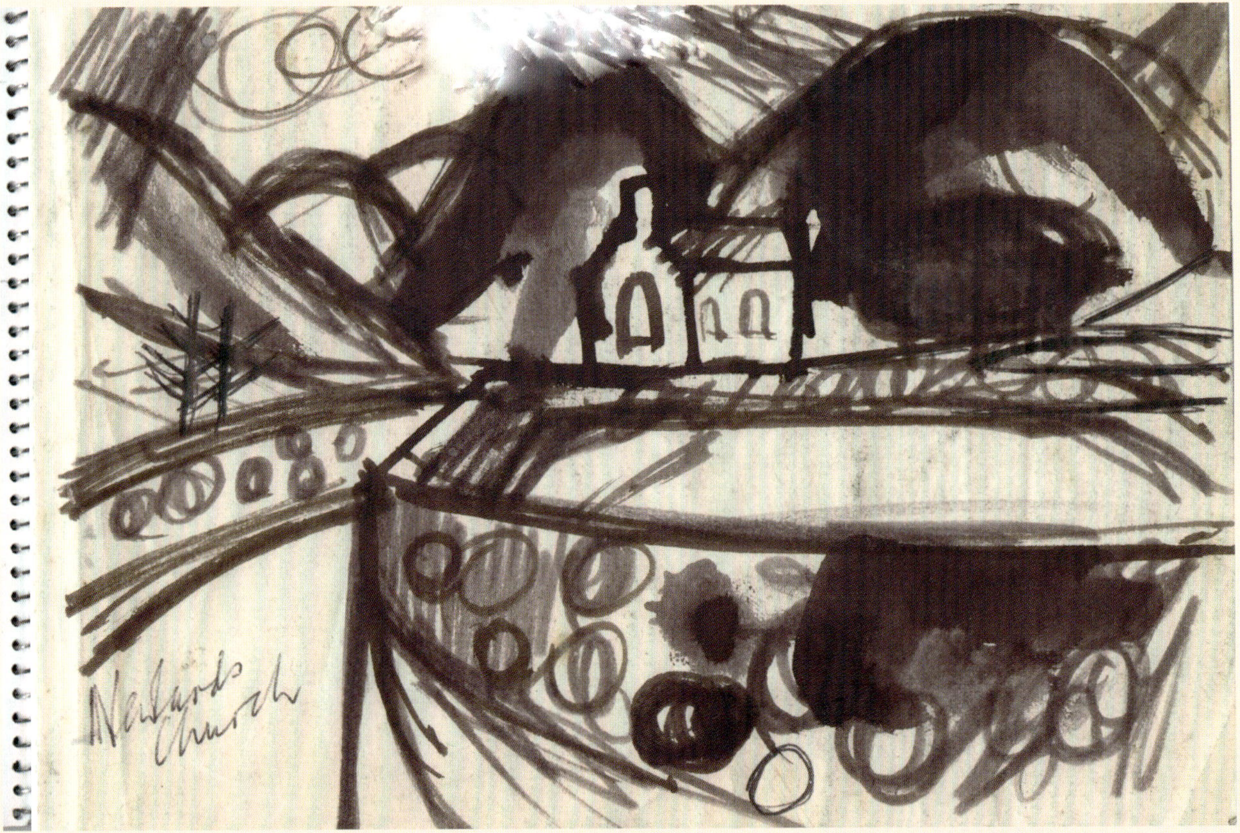

Newlands Church

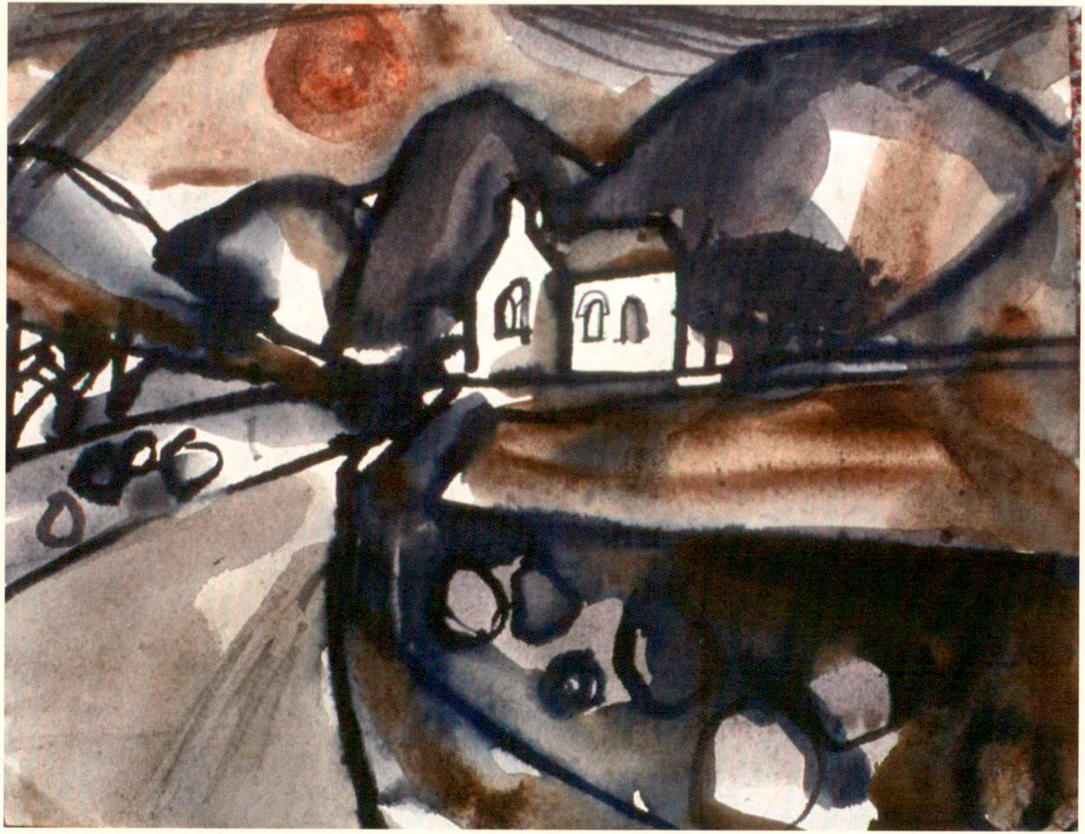

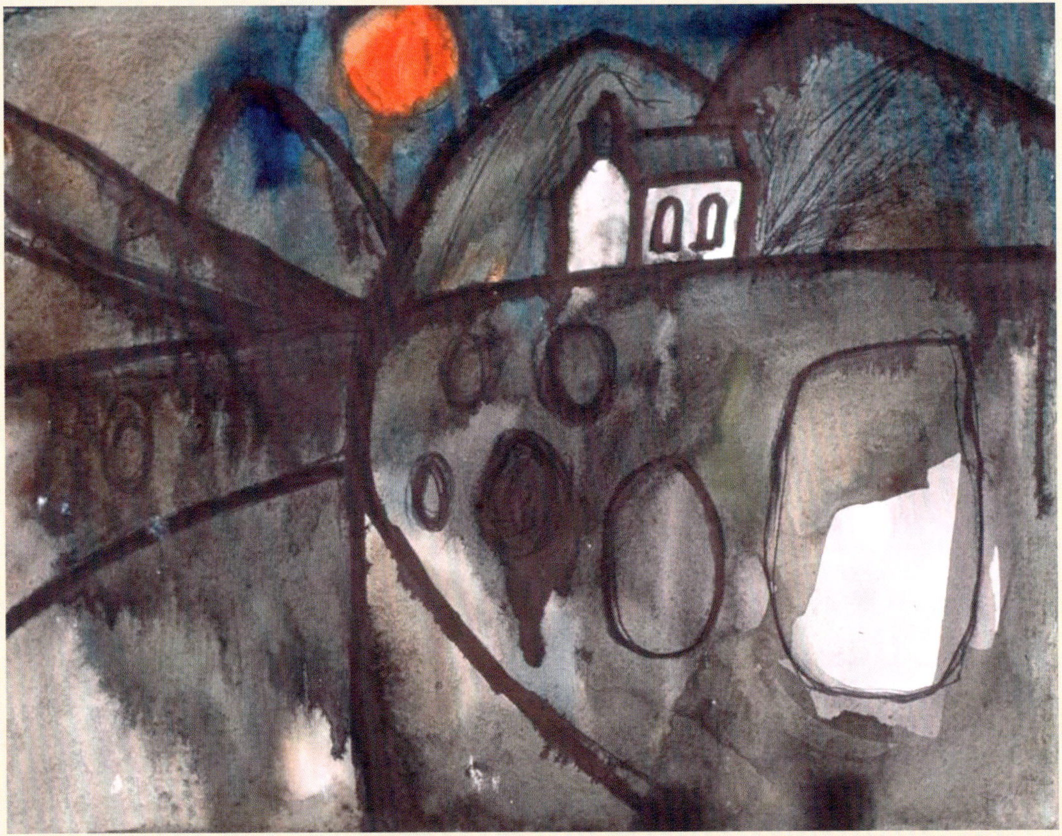

Newlands Church painting

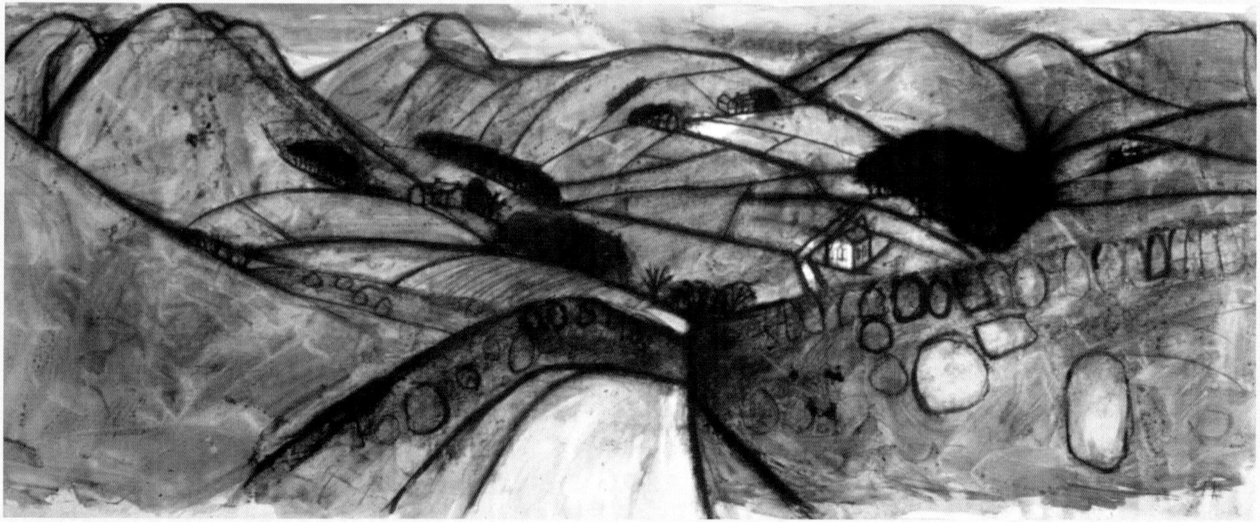

Newlands Valley 78″ x 30″ Charcoal and watercolour.

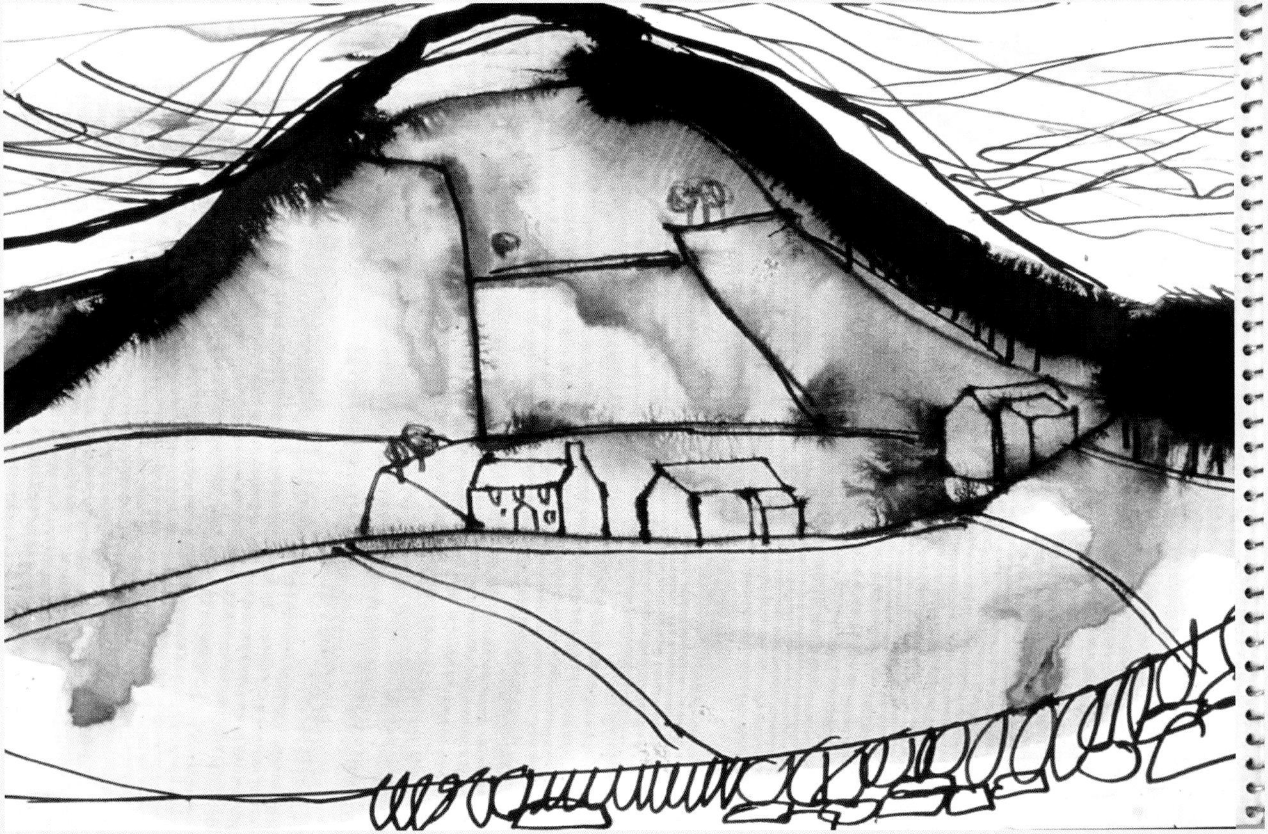

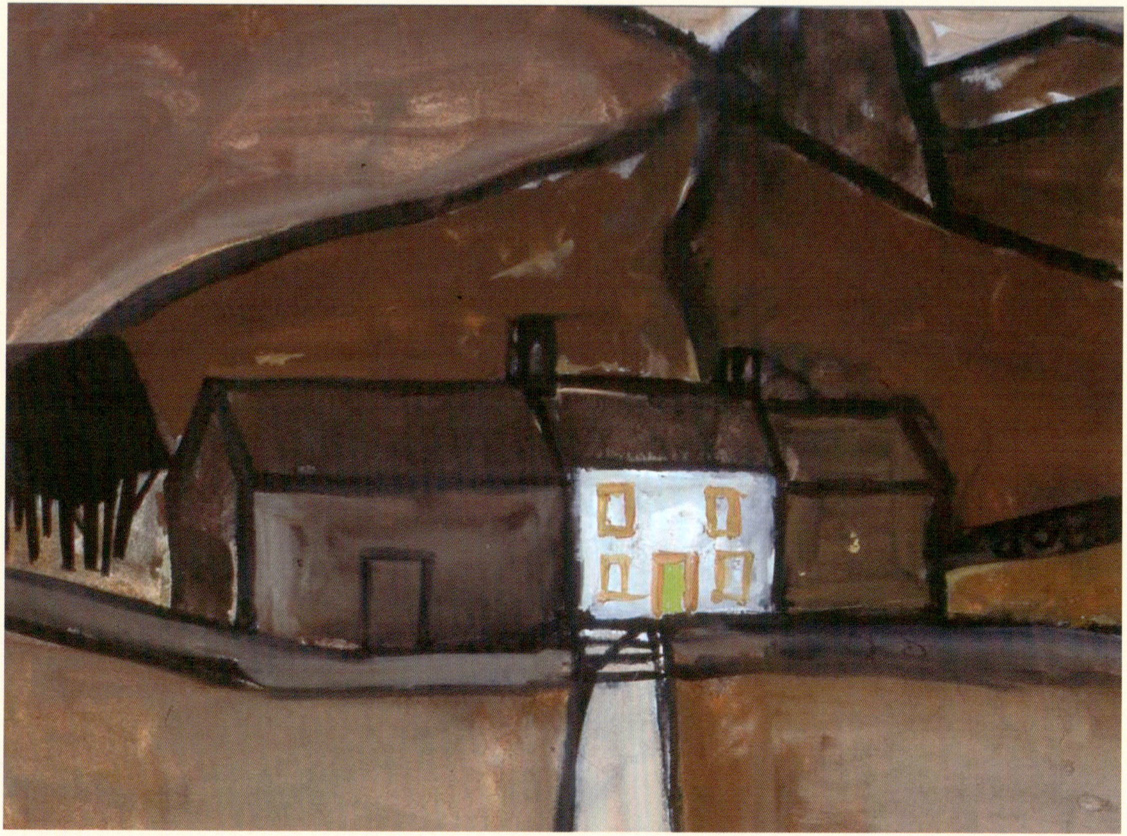

Hill farm

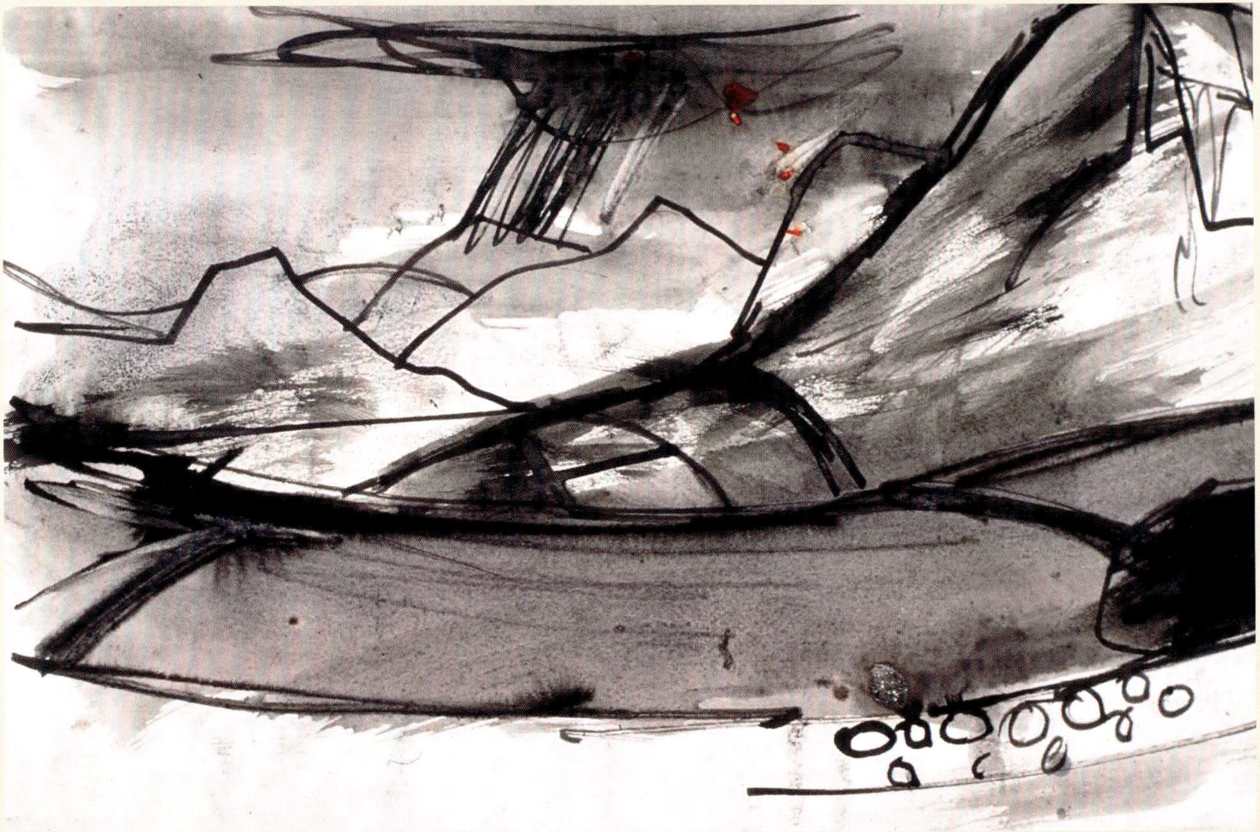

Sketch towards Buttermere from Loweswater

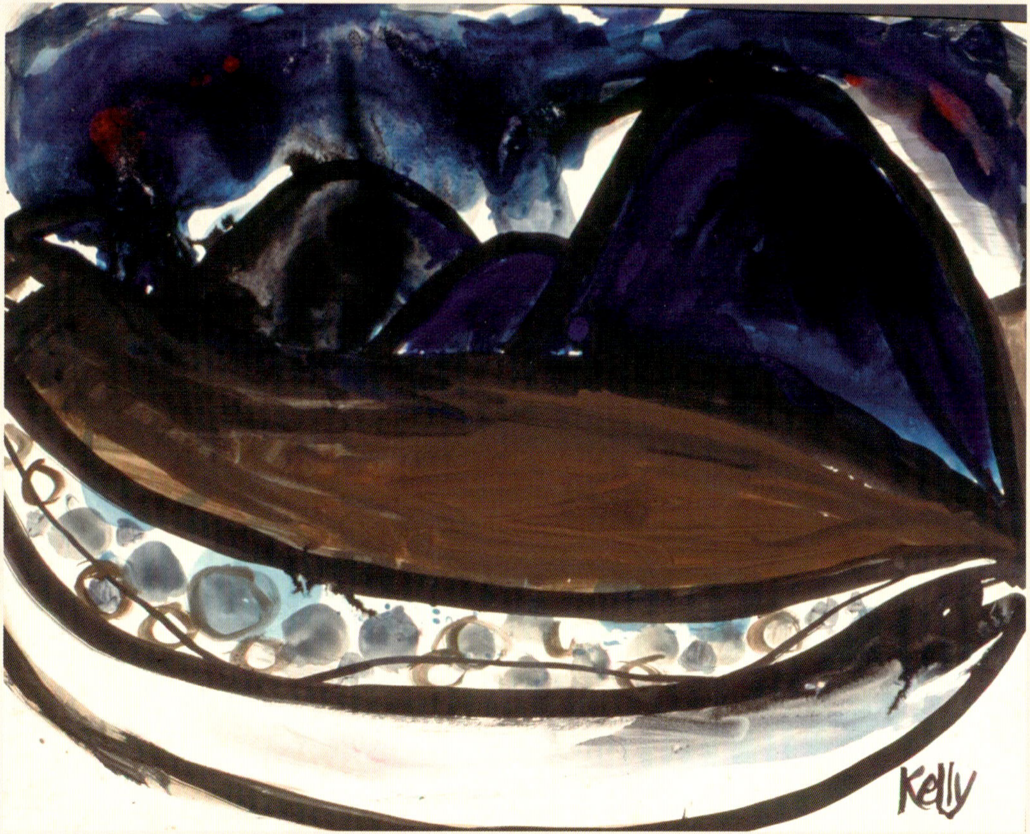

The only painting found signed Kelly rather than PK or Percy Kelly. There is a marked difference in style.

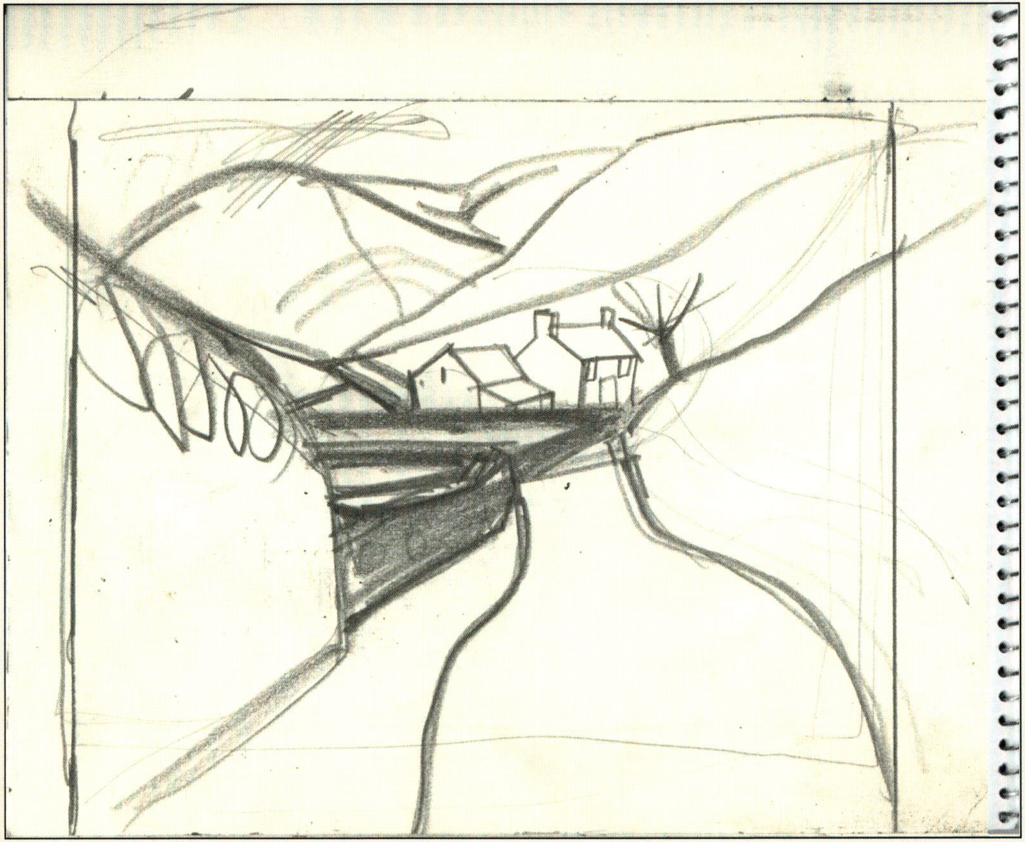

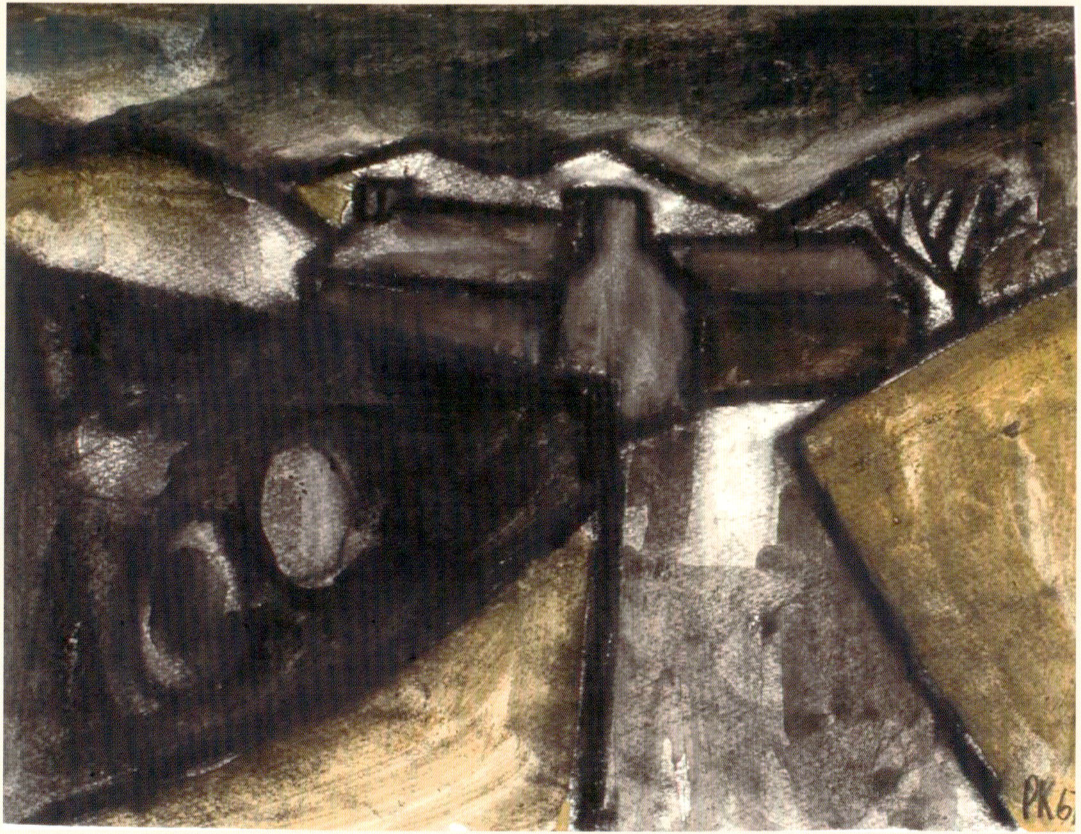

Cumberland landscape 1967

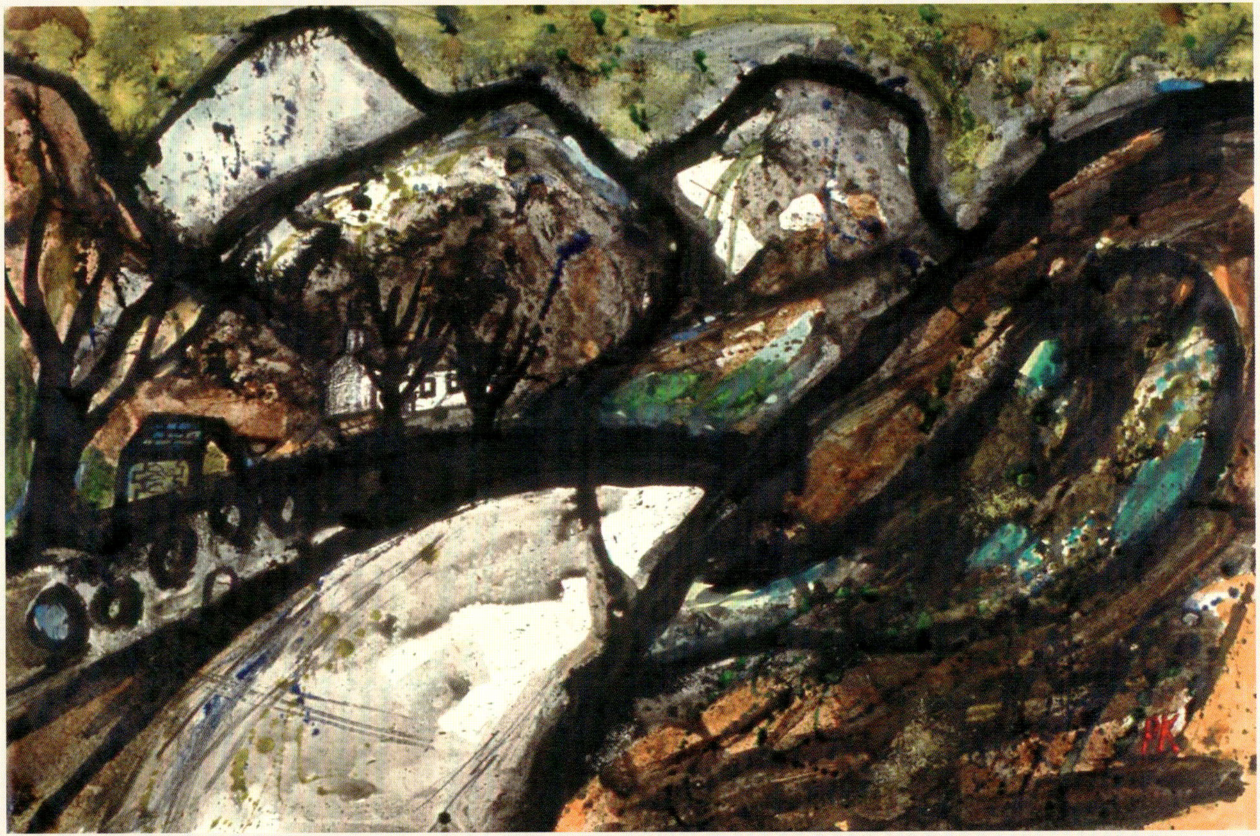

Newlands Valley, executed in expressionist style

WALES - PEMBROKESHIRE

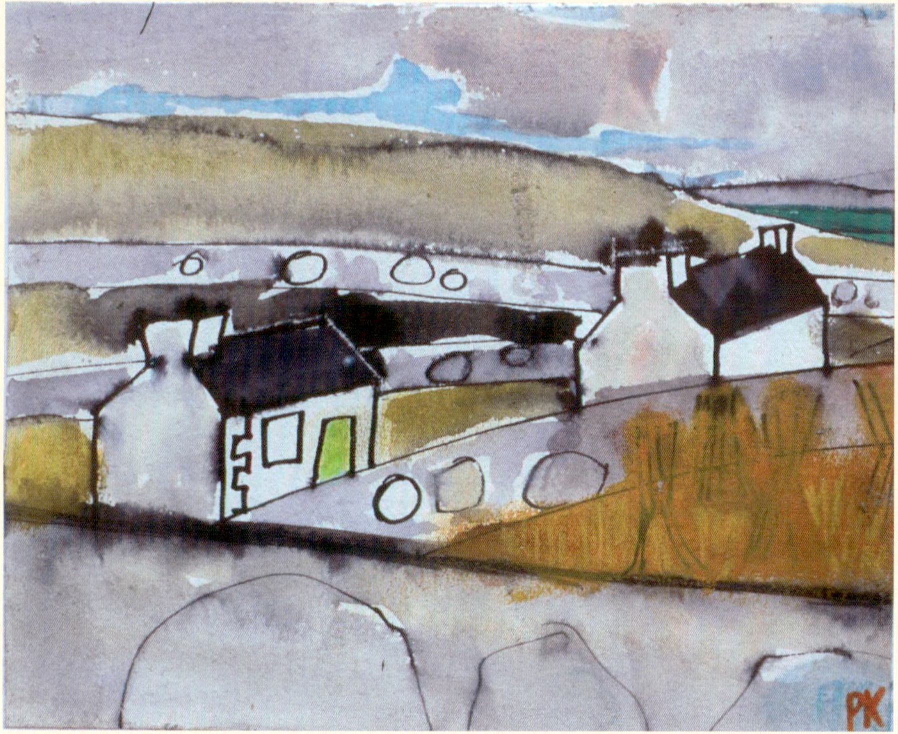

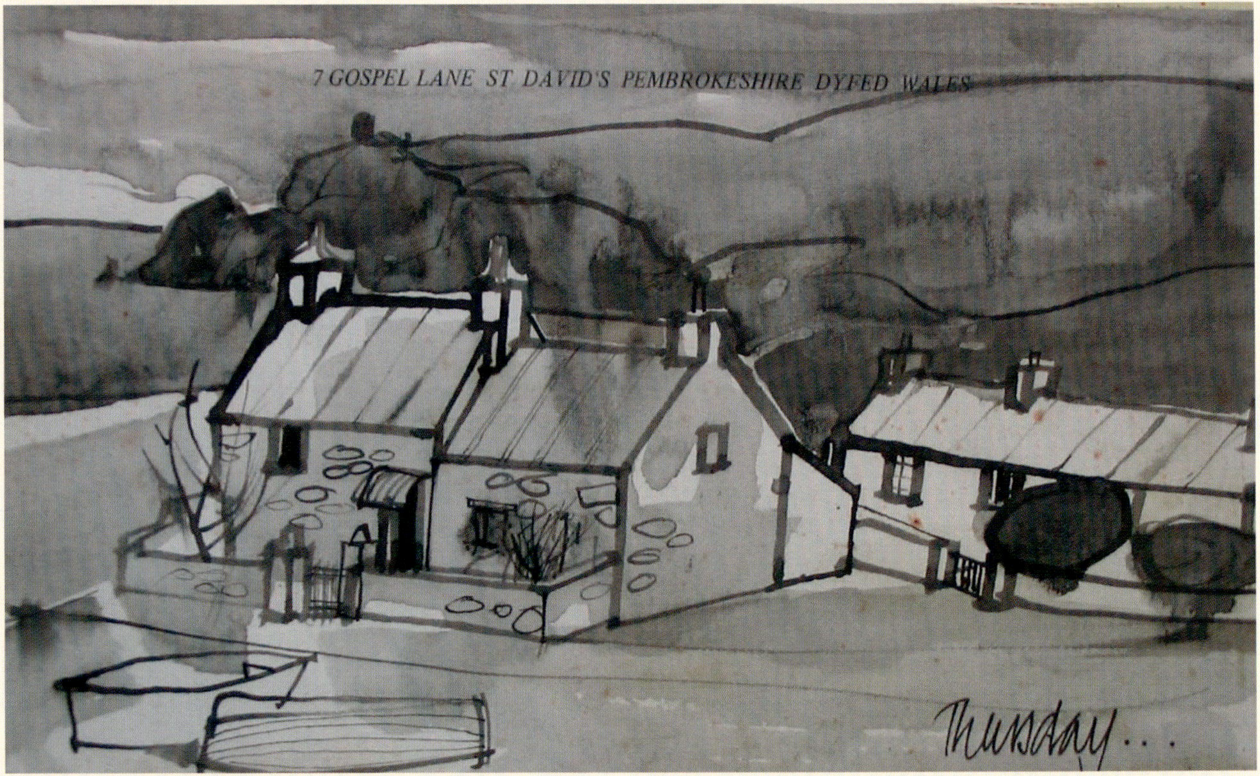

Letterheading St Davids

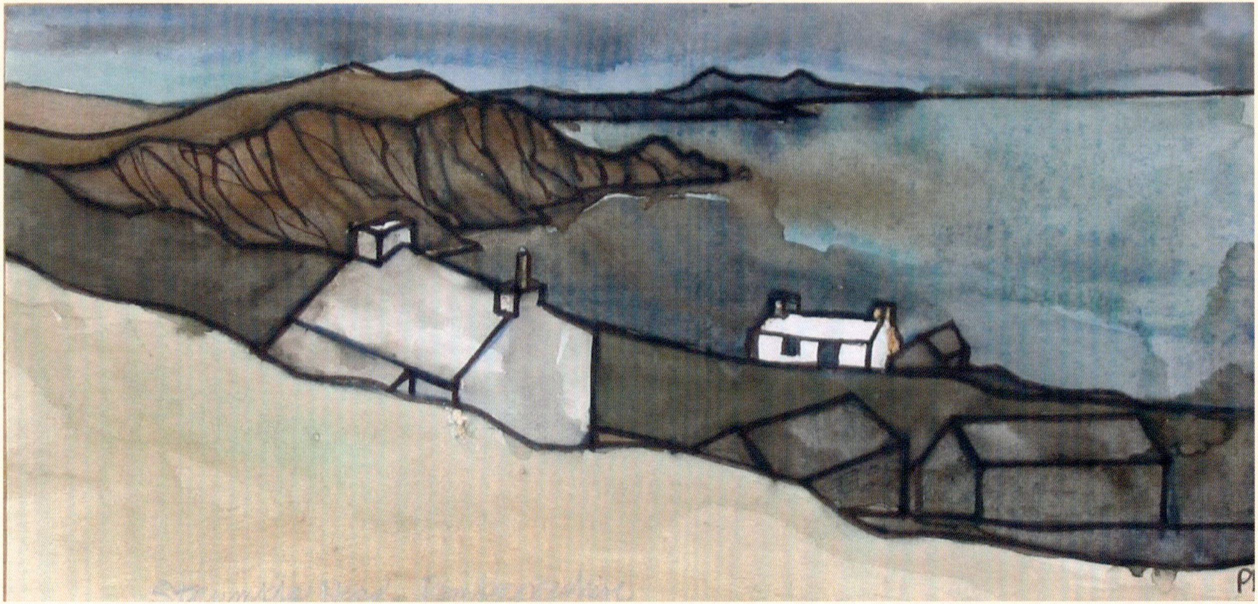

Painting, Strumble Head Watercolour

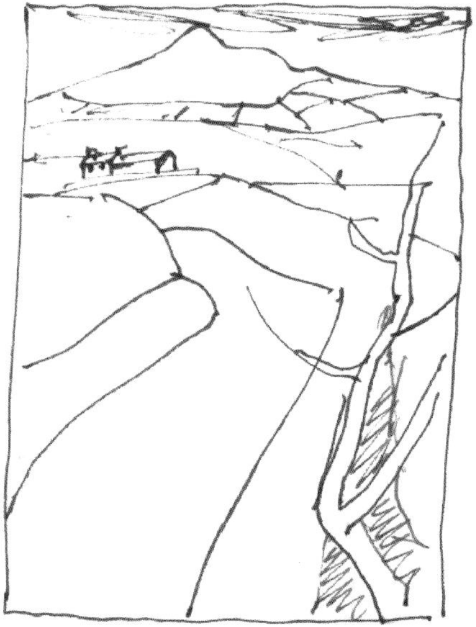

This area quite near to St David's was a favourite place of mine whilst I lived in Pembrokeshire & actually induced me to write some prose for it was a lovely spot. The Road travelled through a bog which was an ever changing variety of colour and texture — way in the distance the fields on the slopes of the rocky hill were very tiny and reminiscent of Brittany & Cornwall. Such a lovely pattern of different greens. at any season. Some yellow corn in the late summer. I always endeavoured to visit the area alone.

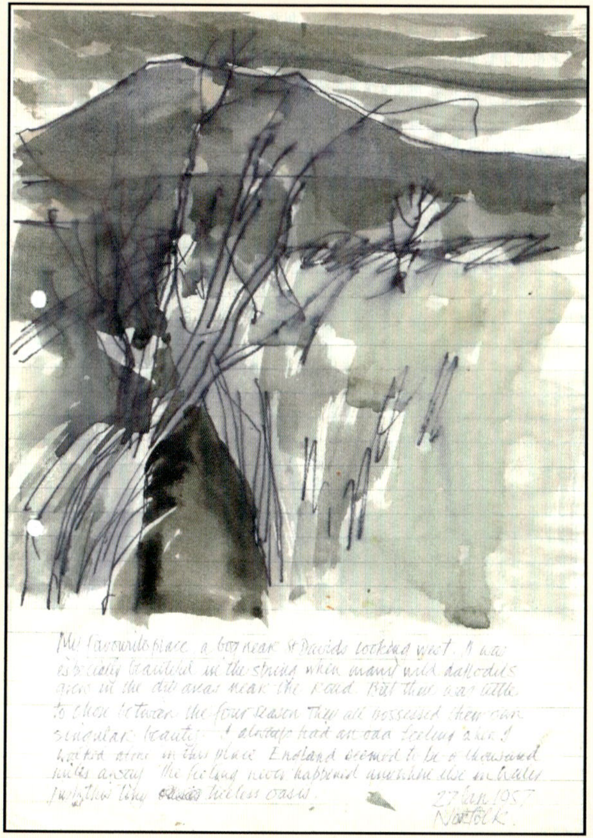

My favourite place, a bog near St Davids looking west. It was especially beautiful in the spring when many wild daffodils grew in the dry areas near the road. But there was little to choose between the four seasons. They all posessed their own singular beauty. I always had an odd feeling when I walked alone in that place. England seemed to be a thousand miles away. The feeling never happened anywhere else in Wales, just in this tiny treeless oasis.

27th Jan 1987

Norfolk

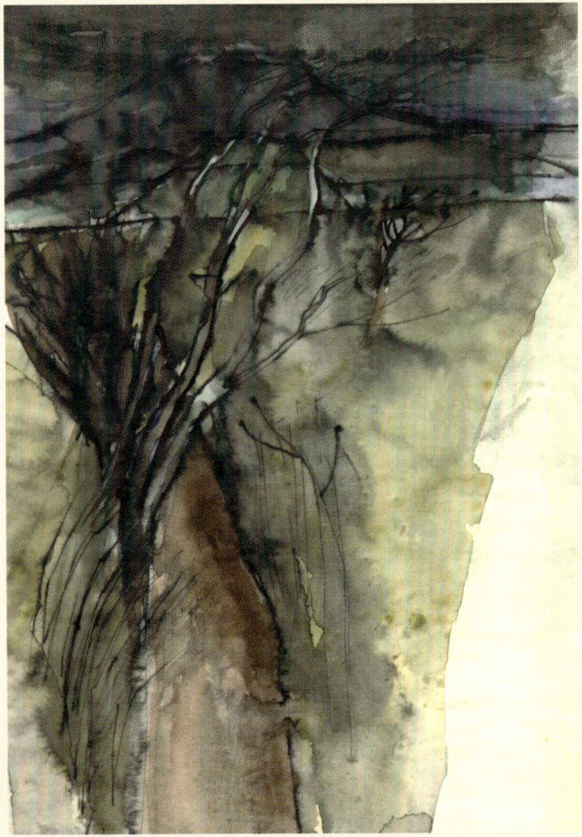

Bog Pembrokeshire

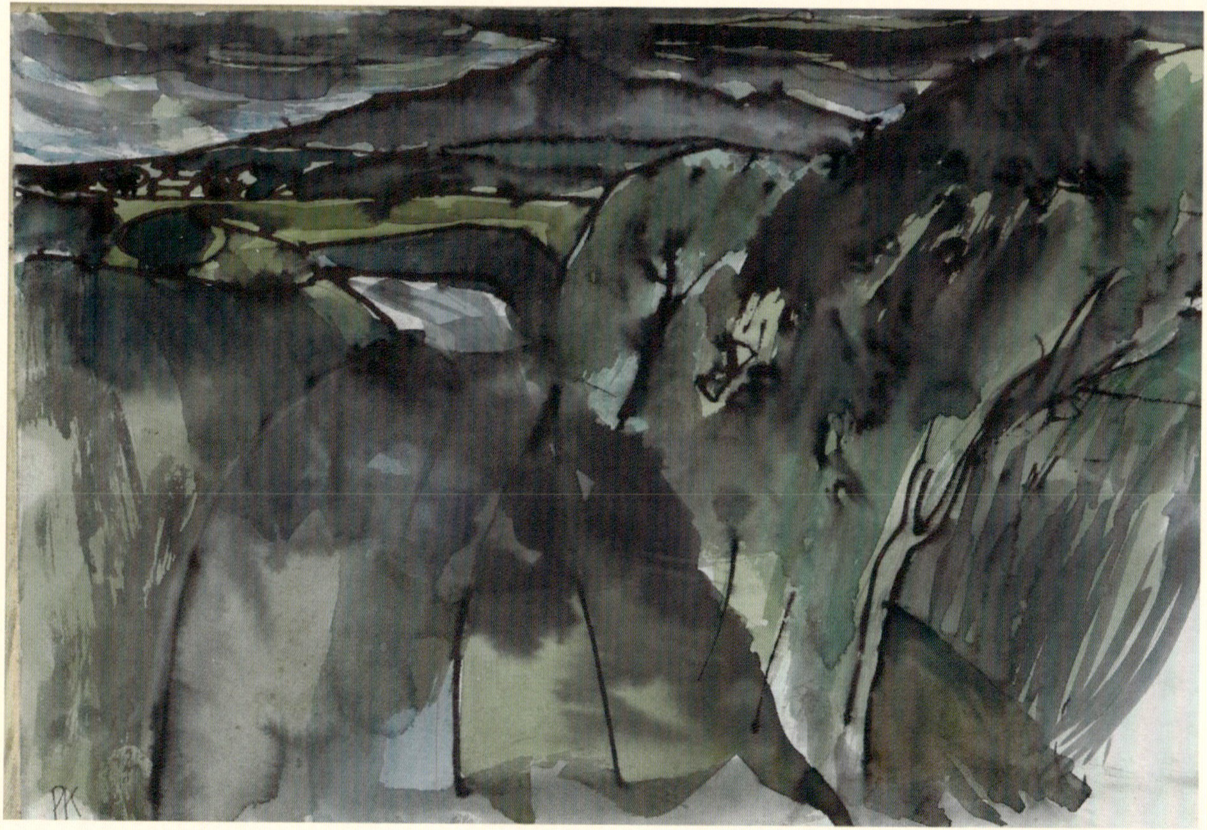

Hedgerows on the bog road, Pembrokeshire

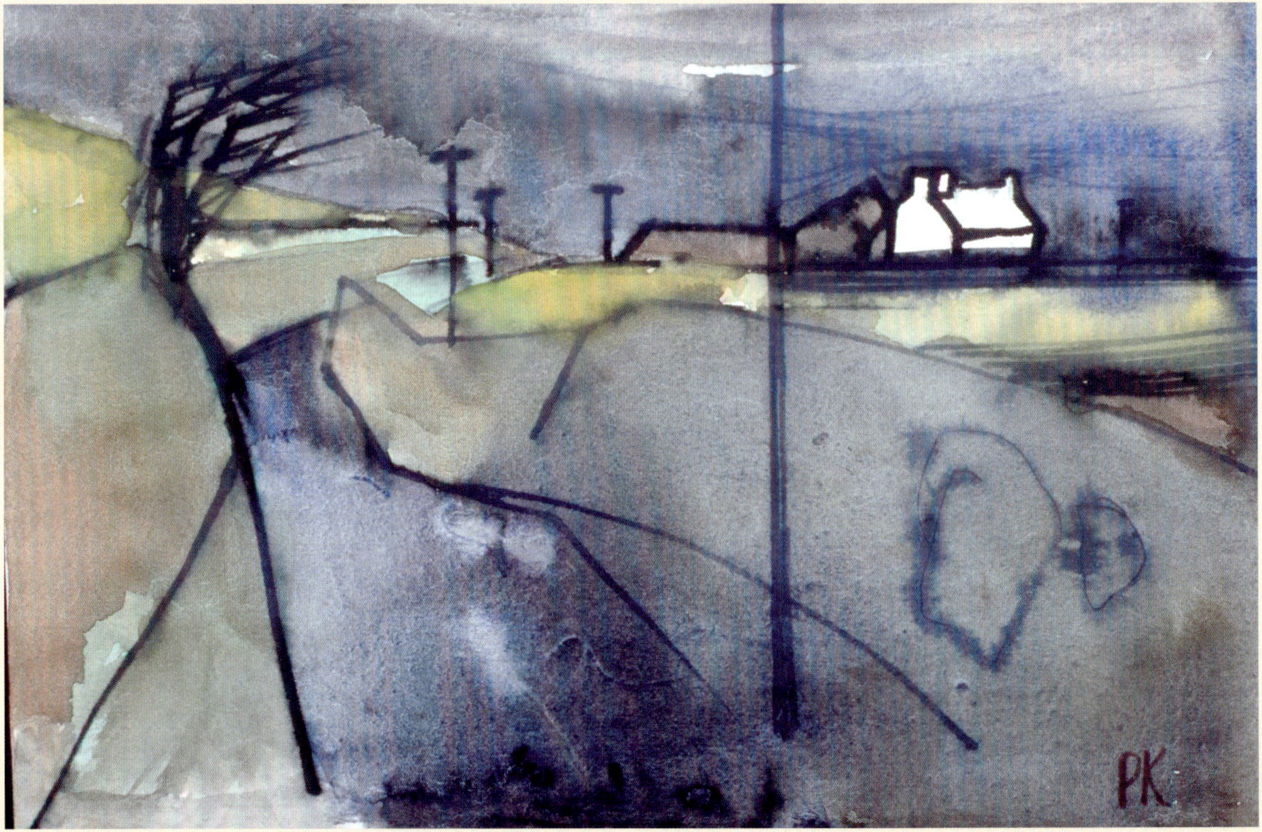

Pembrokeshire lane, Watercolour

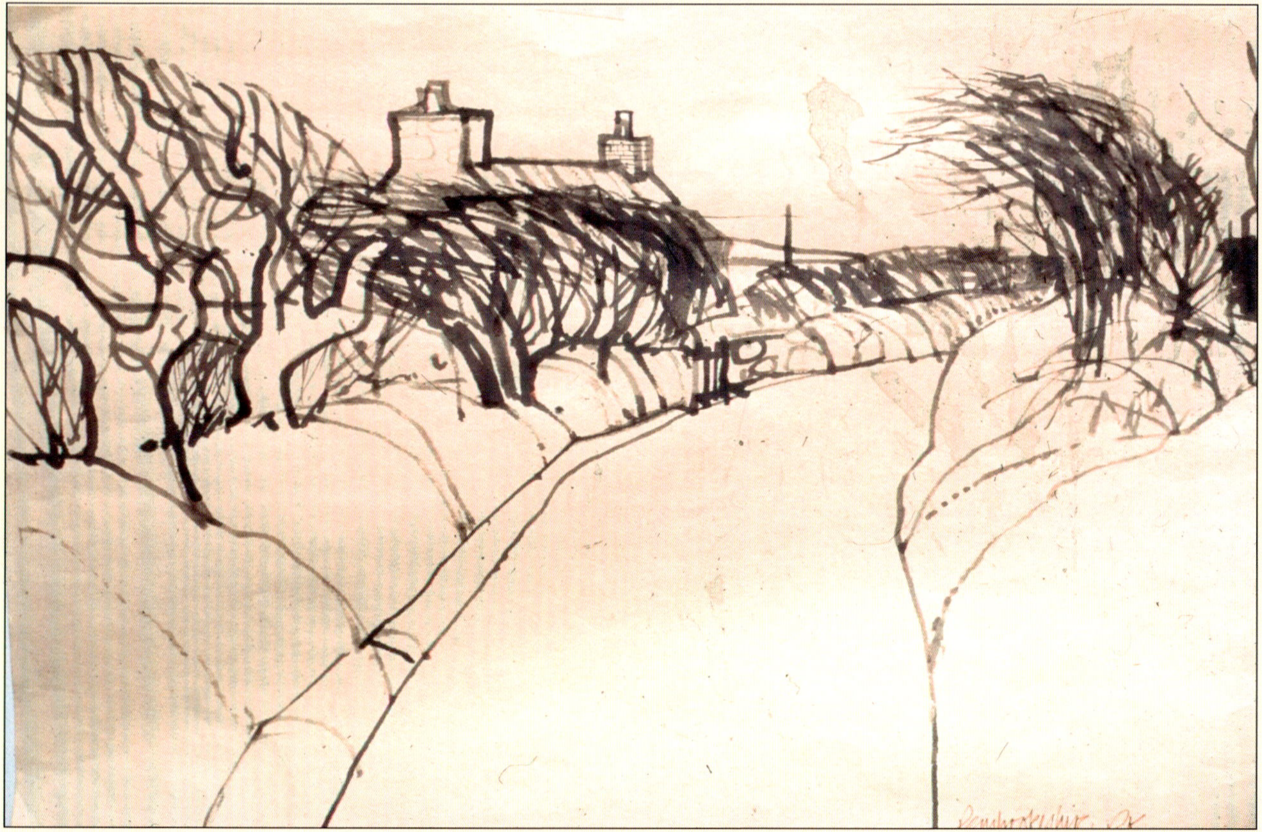

From the Pembrokeshire sketchbook

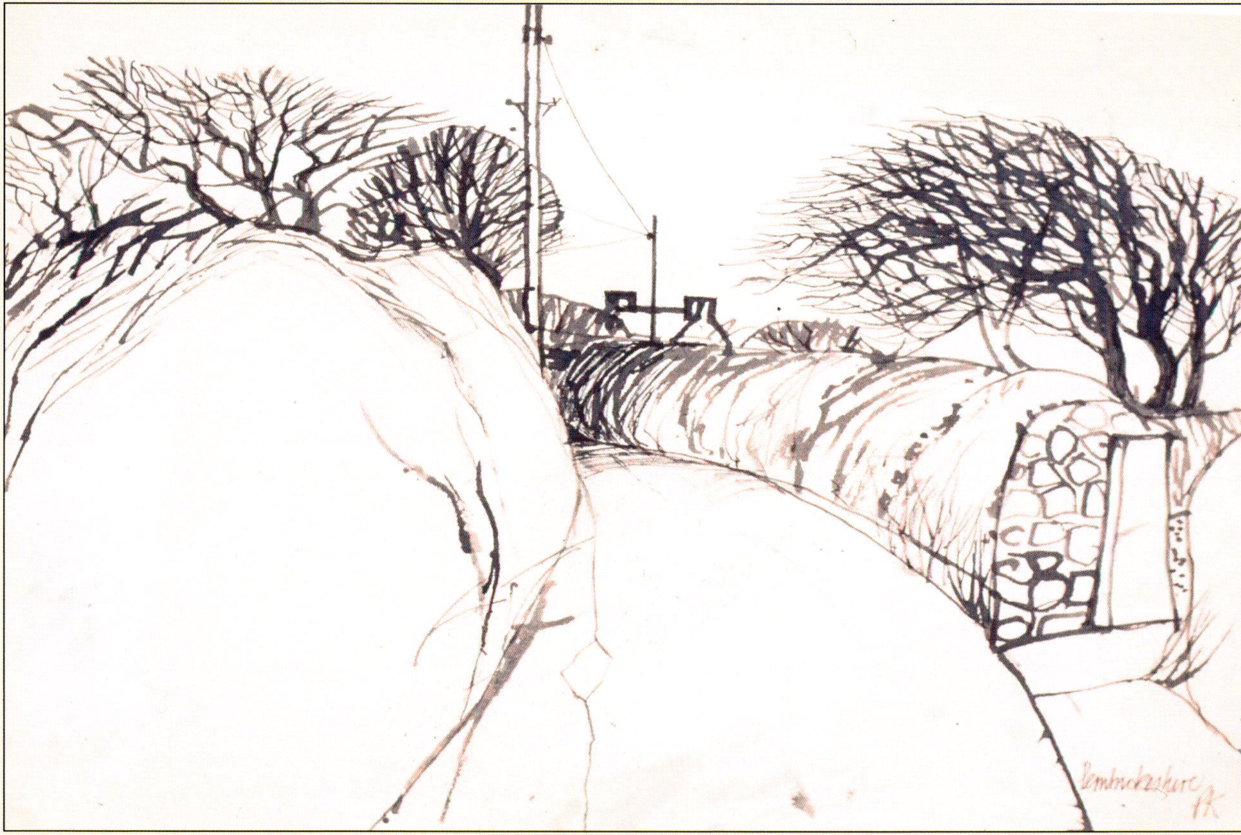

Pembrokeshire

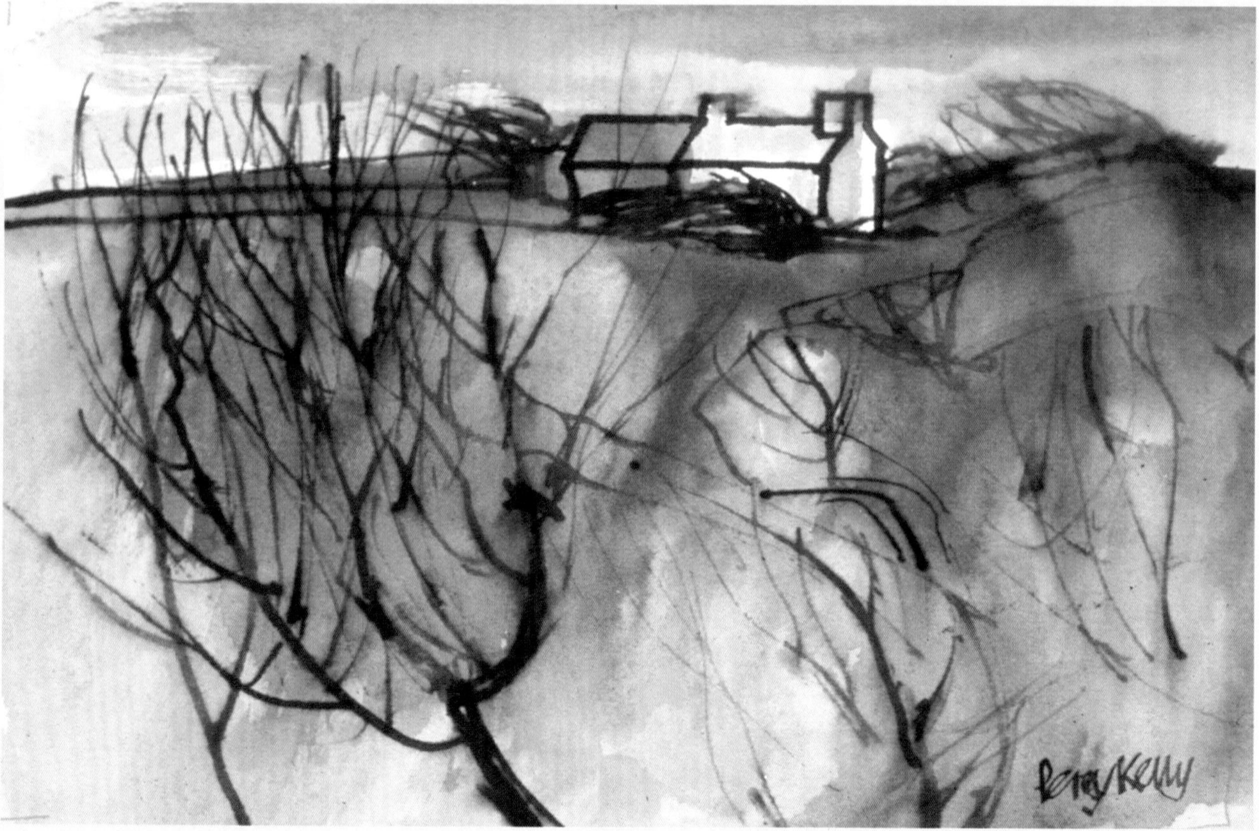

Windy Day

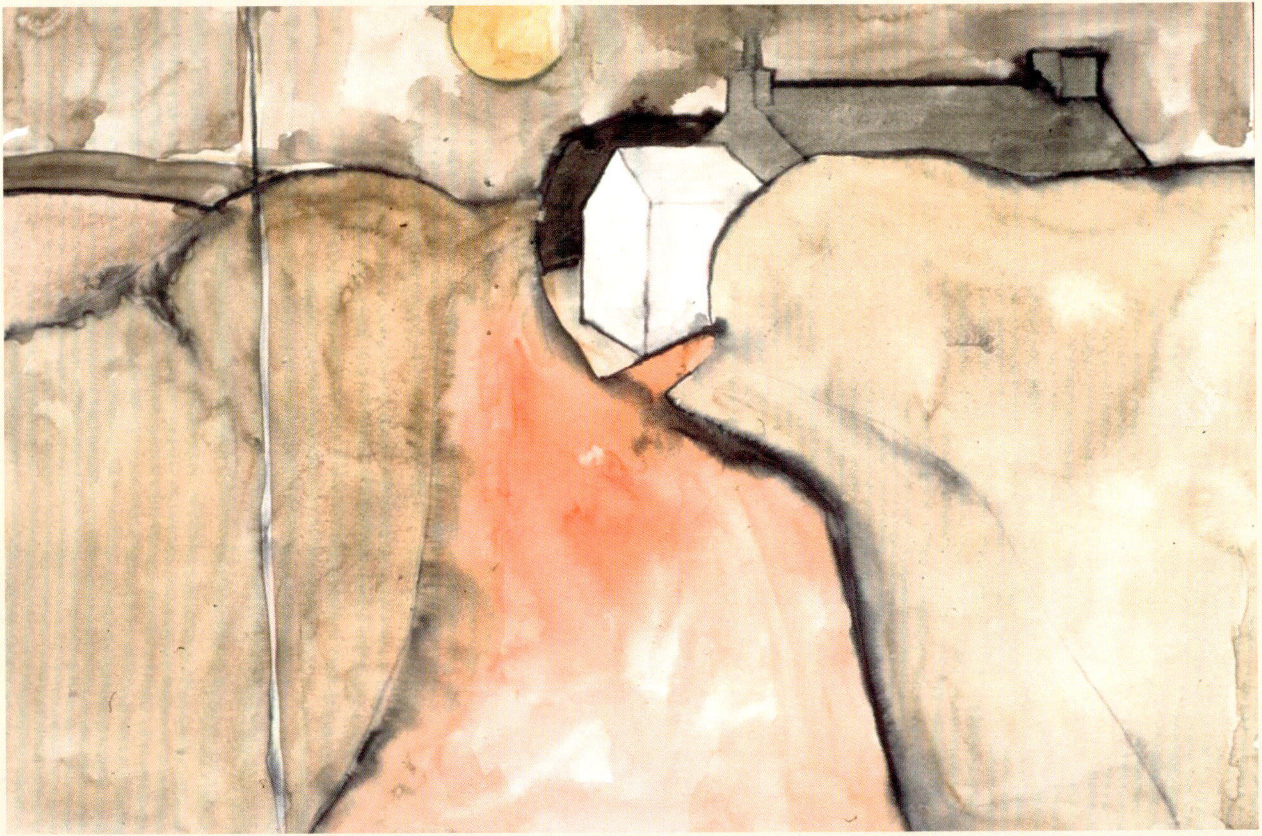

Sketch of Pembrokeshire lane

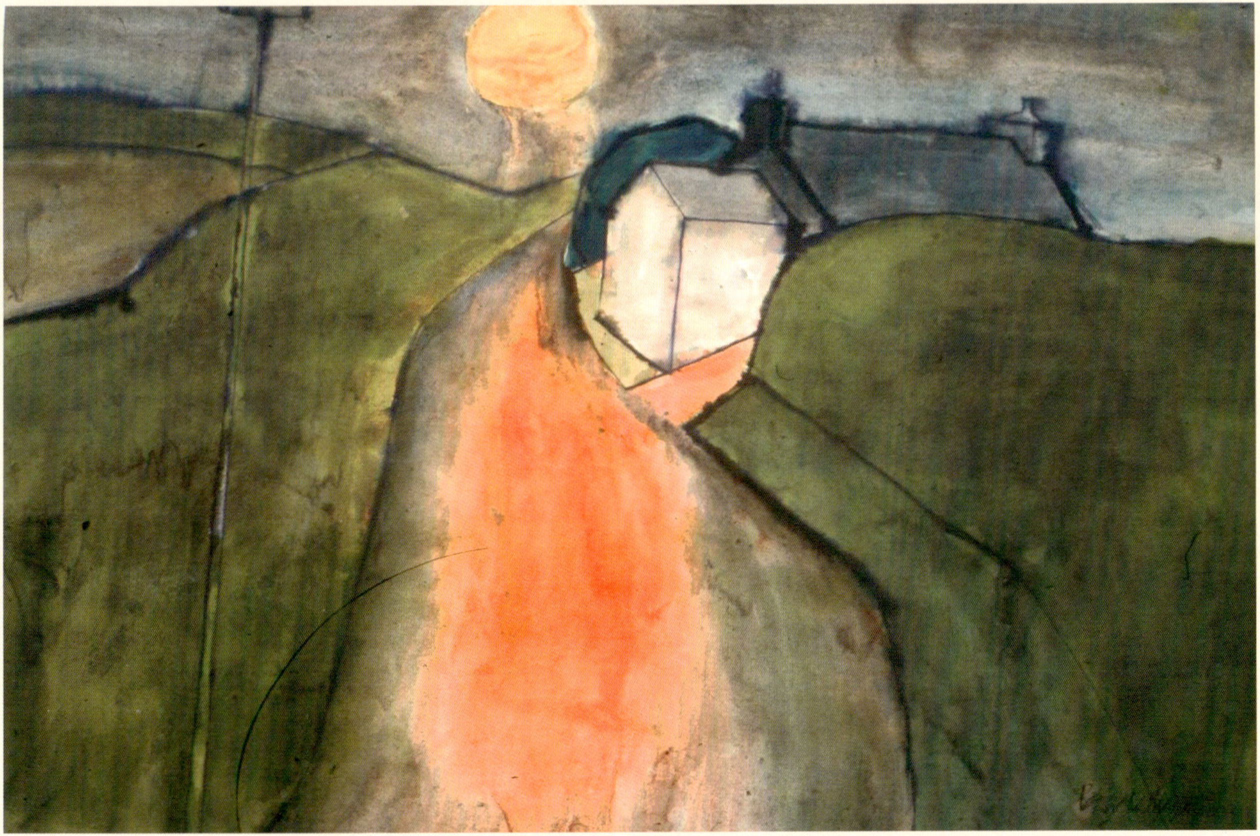

Cottage at sunset watercolour painting

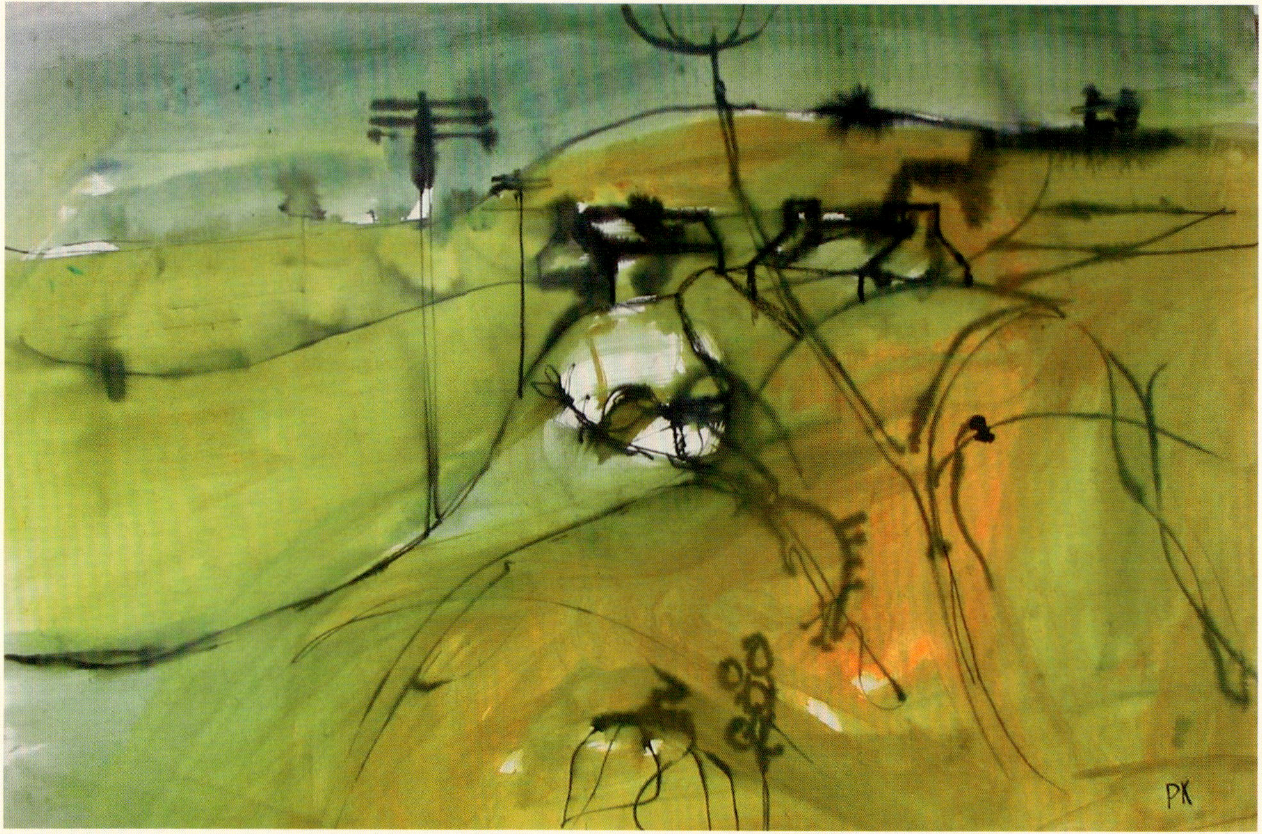
PK

NORFOLK

Kelly's last and loneliest days were in Rockland St Peter in Norfolk where his time was spent surviving after his second wife left him until his death in 1993. With his ongoing car maintenance and building projects as well as his gender confusion, he appears to have done very little sketching. Most of his creative efforts went into the thousands of illustrated letters he sent to Joan David and other friends, as well as using his earlier Cumberland sketches and drawings to make paintings of his favourite places.

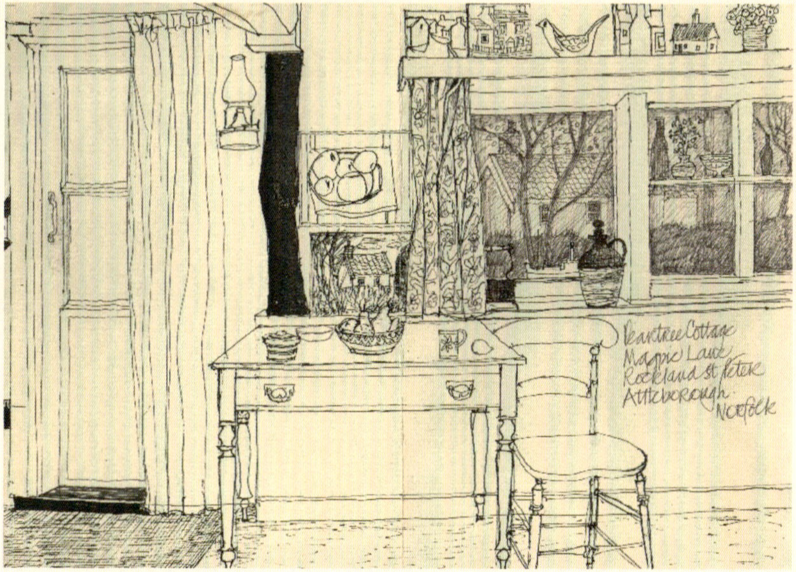

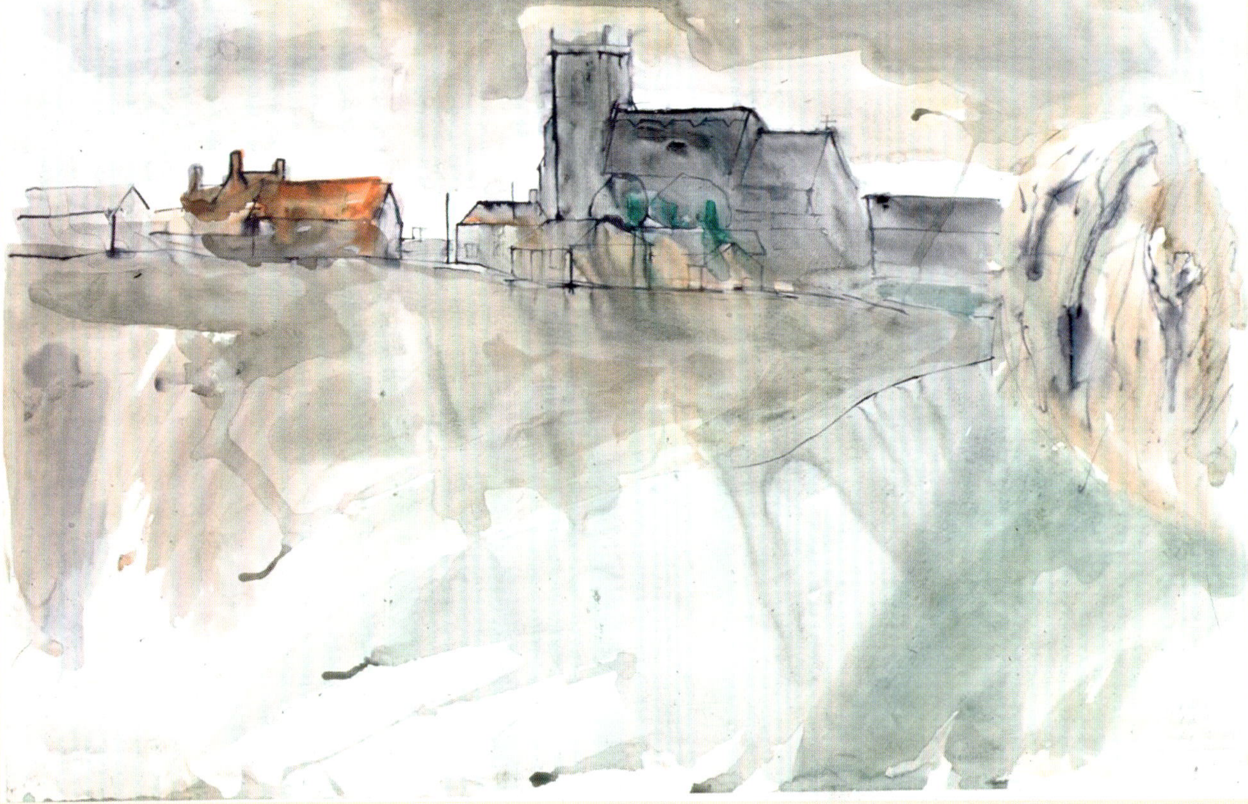

In 1981 Percy made this watercolour sketch while being filmed for Anglia Television.

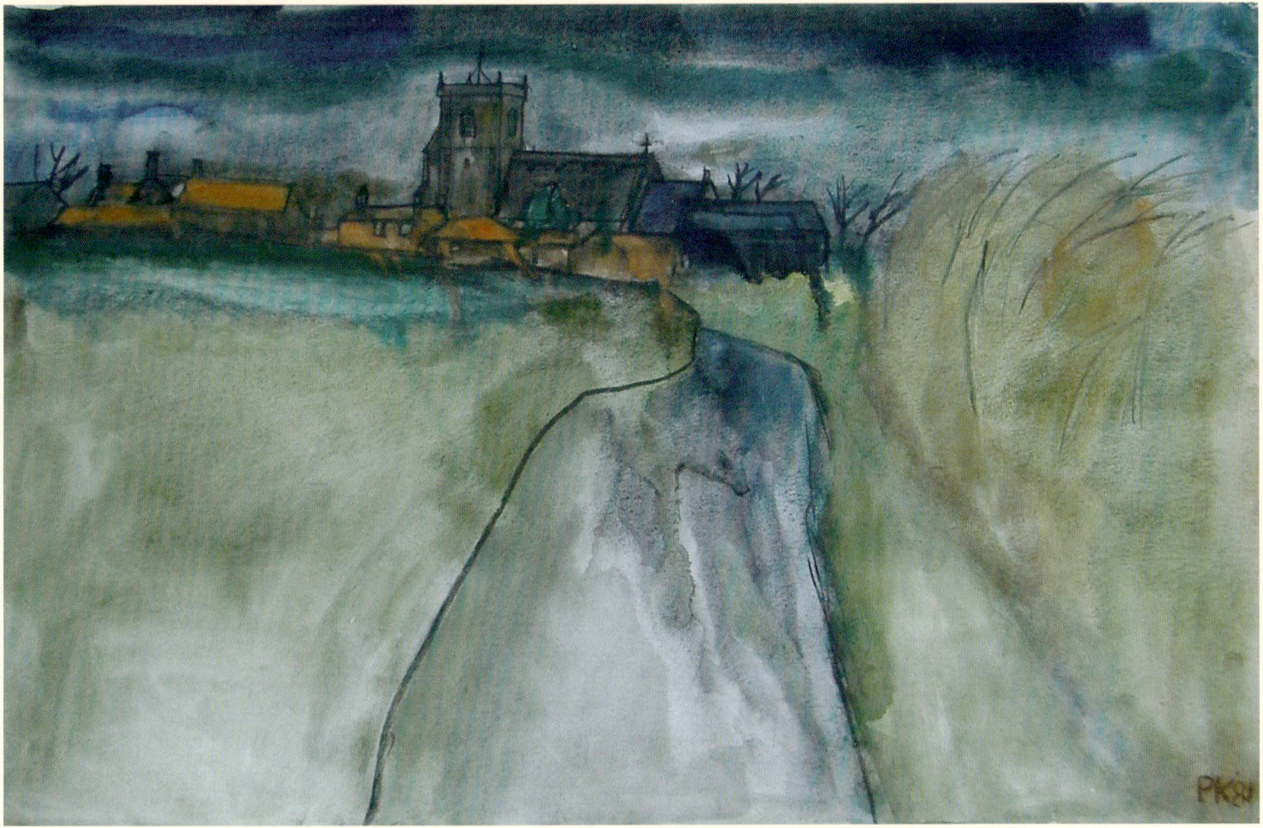

Caston Church watercolour painting made subsequently

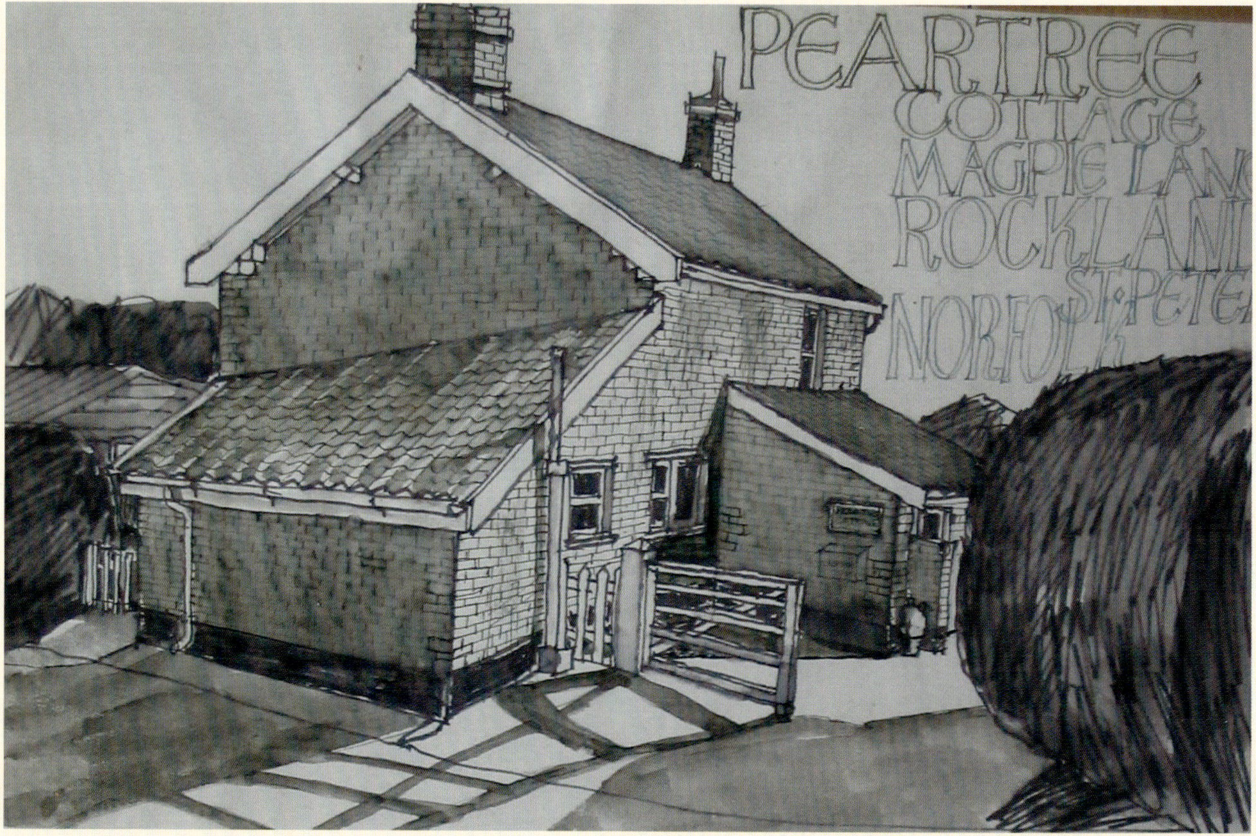
PEARTREE
COTTAGE
MAGPIE LAN
ROCKLAND
ST. PETE
NORFOLK

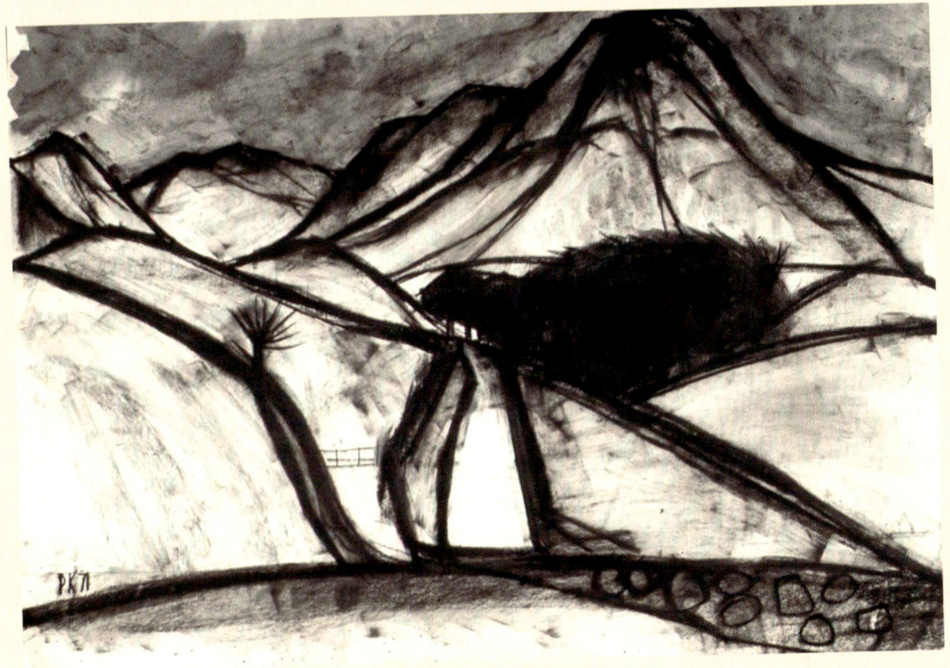

I would dearly love to be transported to the shores of Loweswater. But now I am alone, could I bear the beauty of the place?

Percy Kelly writing to Joan David from Norfolk before his death in 1993

Silent dark and
restless umber

- LOVELY -

gre
ng
sedge stained
ochre brown

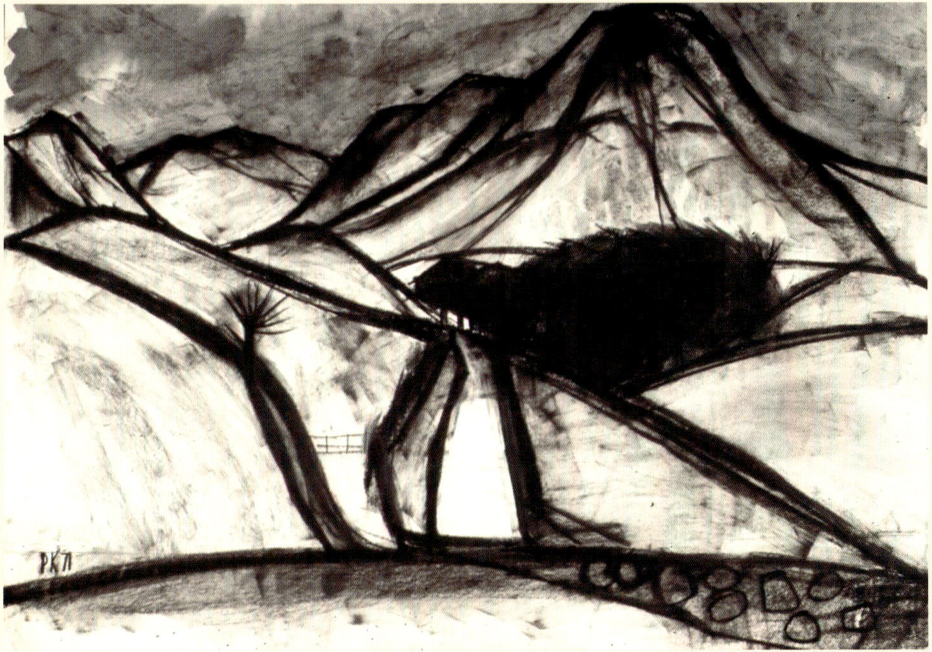

I would dearly love to be transported to the shores of Loweswater. But now I am alone, could I bear the beauty of the place?

Percy Kelly writing to Joan David from Norfolk before his death in 1993

Silent dark and
restless umber
gre ng
sedge stained
ochre brown

- LOVELY -